# The Real Deal

## What young people really think about government, politics and social exclusion

Written by Tom Bentley and Kate Oakley
with Sîan Gibson and Kylie Kilgour

 CAMELOT Foundation    DEMOS    **Centrepoint** Housing young people at risk    pilotlight    **Save the Children**    in association with  NCVO voice of the voluntary sector

Published in 1999 by
Demos
Panton House
25 Haymarket
London
SW1Y 4EN

ISBN 1 898 309 83 3

Printed in Great Britain by Redwood Books
Cover design by Matthew Cooper
Text design by Lindsay Nash

# Contents

## Acknowledgements

First and most important, thanks to the young people who participated in the Real Deal. Their commitment, honesty and talent made the project a success.

Thanks to all those who organised, contributed to and supported the project:

Group workers: Richard Barber, Carol Nevison, Nicola Chapman, Robert MacFarlane, Bridgit Pettit, Jenny Dagg, Anna Whalen, Rahman Karim, Phil Tresider, Paula Rodgers, Siobhan Molloy, Goretti Horgan, Susan Elsley, Linda Dawson, Sheila Wood, Dod Forrest, Lynn Wotherspoon, Una Murray, Kathryn Potter, Rhona Kennedy, Kylie Kilgour. Project steering group: Madeleine Tearse, Cathy Havell, Yolande Burgin, Julia Brown, Vanessa Howe, Richard Warner, Tom Bentley. Communications group: Debbie Porter, Tom Hampson, Lisa Mangan, Leigh Daynes: Researchers: Kate Oakley, Husna Mortuza, Ben Jupp.

Thanks also to Perpetua Kirby, Kirsten Walton, Jane Tewson, Richard Lewis and Sarah Macauley, and to the many other people who supported and contributed to the project.

# Executive summary

The Real Deal is a unique project, consulting over 150 young people over eight months about their views of politics, social exclusion and the government policies that affect them. These young people have, between them, direct experience of the most severe forms of disadvantage, adversity and exclusion from mainstream society. They know at first hand what it is like to experience homelessness, the care system, abuse, school exclusion, drugs, unemployment and family conflict. Where these issues are concerned, they are the experts. But most had *never* been consulted before about their views.

The Real Deal set out to discover these young people's views and create opportunities to present them directly to policy-makers. During fringe meetings at the Party conferences, and a policy seminar at 11 Downing Street, young people gave their views, made policy recommendations and debated the issues with senior politicians and civil servants.

The full report sets out the results of group discussions, individual interviews, seminars and public debates. It explains the context and methodology of the project and makes detailed policy recommendations.

## Key findings

These young people are held back by **poverty** and material disadvantage. In particular, their participation in education and training beyond sixteen is made more difficult by lack of financial support. When they are struggling to achieve the basic material conditions of life, it is difficult for them to see why they should be actively involved in politics and community life.

> *At the end of the day, the reason why most of us don't vote is that we are homeless and unemployed. We are trying to get ourselves some money and a permanent place to live, a job. We are too busy doing other things that are more important in our lives than voting. I don't really care who runs the country, as long as things are made fair.*

The pressures of living in a market-oriented, media-driven society are just as great for these young people as for anyone else. Their experience of multiple disadvantages make these pressures even harder to cope with.

*Everything's more appealing now, faster cars and that, and the young'uns do not get nay money, but there's better stuff like computers so there's more burglaries and car crime.*

These young people are alienated from mainstream **politics** and distrustful of politicians in general. They feel that they are labelled and discriminated against by adult society.

*Yeah, but our class we are just a statistic but like with upper classes what they say matters with all the politicians, they are higher up in class so what they vote for counts, more closer to them.*

*I don't think it's going to make any difference to a young homeless irrelevant person like me, I'm not going to make any difference.*

These young people do not recognise the conventional definition of **community**, seeing it as sentimental and irrelevant. Community is important to them, but is seen as those who have common views and experiences. These young people feel a strong need for mutual care and support, but many feel that 'communities' are a source of interference and control.

*The weird thing about being an outsider in a community is that it feels like everything is going on somewhere else.*

*I fought … to make it in this world. You have got to make it for yourself. There is no community willing to help you … not that they can't, there are the resources there to help you if want to but they don't.*

Despite the severity of some of their experiences, these young people have the same **aspirations** in life as most other people. They want homes, jobs and families.

At the same time, in keeping with the rest of their generation, they want to be respected and recognised as individuals, and not labelled or judged for their youth, their dress or their interests.

*I'd like to complete college, get a nice job, be integrated into society and just lead a normal life.*

Some found it hard to think beyond the struggle of the present:

*I just think about how I'm going to get through this day. I don't think about next week or two weeks or whatever.*

**Education** is fundamentally important. Many feel let down by the education system, but most still see learning as vital. Education should concentrate more on practical and emotional skills. Schools and teachers should be better able to respond to other problems in young people's lives.

*I think you go to school at the wrong time. It's set for the wrong age. When you are at school, I don't know about anybody else, but I never wanted to be there. But now I would quite happily go to school.*

*School? Totally crap. I learnt nothing of much use there. It just taught you to have no respect for teachers or the system.*

These young people recognise that the **world of work** has changed, but their experience of work is mostly harsh and negative. Few had experienced stable long-term employment. Most had worked in the informal or illegal economies. Many experienced exploitation and under-payment by employers. Many felt that that a balance between work, learning and income was impossible to find.

*Yeah, it used to be much more "you'll definitely have a job for life and a house for life" and it's a lot different from that now. You might get a job now but in a week you might be living in a box in the street again.*

**Family** is a fundamental source of influence and support. Many had negative experiences of family life, but this did not stop them from caring about parents and relatives, or from seeing family as an important part of their aspirations for the future.

*I want to have good relationships with people. I want to have a better relationship with my children than my mother has with me, because although I admire her and I respect her a lot, we're not really close. That's it.*

The process of achieving **independence** through adulthood was a difficult and uncertain one. For those who experienced the care system, bridges between care and independence were inadequate. For young people in the Traveller community, marriage is the point at which you reach adulthood. For others, there is no one point. Adulthood was seen more as a state of mind than as an age or formal status.

*I don't think you are ever really independent. Everybody needs somebody. It's so hard when you're so young. I was sixteen. You can't get a decent wage. I'll always be dependent on somebody. I don't want to be totally independent.*

These young people see themselves as **offering solutions**. Many felt that their negative experiences could be used to help them, and others, to face the future. Many have experience of taking responsibility for themselves and others at an early age. This should be seen as a resource rather than a barrier.

Services and support for young people need to become more personalised, flexible and responsive to what they say about their needs. Better information about what is available should also be a priority.

*I think, I mean just getting in, I've managed to get into the system. I think there's a lot of help to be done in just getting people into it. I mean I've spent a couple of years completely outside it all, didn't exist as far as anybody was concerned. And I mean now I'm on the road to getting where I want to go. And once you get into services and you find out and connect to one thing you can connect to everything, but if you never connect to the first part then you never ever reach any of that.*

Above all, these young people want to be respected and they want their views and ideas to be listened to:

*Coming to the Real Deal meetings is the only say we have ever had, like no one has ever asked us about politics before, no teachers, parents or anything like that. This is the only opportunity we have had to talk.*

*If they did a bit more research about what was going on in our heads they would know what else to do instead, if they cared a bit more.*

## Recommendations

### *Support services*

■ Welfare, social and family services should be easier to access. Entitlements from different departments such as housing, social security and employment, should be better linked.

■ Packages of support should be personalised, and guidance and support workers should be able to advise young people as they make progress over time.

■ Professionals, especially teachers and police, should be better trained in listening to and working with young people.

■ Schools should employ confidential counsellors whom young people could confide in. This might include counselling by peers.

■ A package of support and training equivalent to the New Deal should be available for sixteen and seventeen year olds. There should be a flexible gateway period for young people with prevocational needs.

■ Better, more accessible information should be available about opportunities and entitlements for young people.

■ Government should introduce support packages for young people leaving care and home and who are homeless. These should include guidance, follow-up support, peer education and rent deposit schemes.

■ Young people should be involved in evaluating the outcomes and management of support services.

■ Voluntary organisations providing support services to young people should develop more effective forms of user involvement.

## Learning

■ The curriculum should include development of practical and emotional skills which help young people to cope with the situations they face out of school.

■ Work and learning should be better integrated, and learning facilities and support should be available in a wider range of contexts.

■ Young people need better preparation and more sustained support for the transition from school to post-compulsory education and work.

■ Schools should be equipped to respond to problems that young people face in the rest of their lives. Social, family and educational services should be better integrated. Systems of pastoral care and support need greater priority.

## Work

■ Benefits entitlements should be suspended rather than cancelled when a young person takes up temporary work.

■ Careers guidance and work experience should be drastically improved to make them more relevant and should be introduced earlier in young people's educational careers.

■ The minimum wage and other in-work benefits should be monitored to ensure that they do not discriminate against young people.

■ Childcare places should be more widely available. There should be ongoing support for young parents and carers.

## Supporting safe lifestyles

■ Government policy on drugs should reflect the reality of young people's lives and focus on a harm reduction model. The legalisation of cannabis should be debated widely. More accurate, relevant information about drugs should be widely available.

■ There should be a wider range of safe, interesting places for young people to socialise and learn. Young people should be involved in managing and providing services for others. Support and listening services should also be available at these venues.

■ Government should examine strategies for improving concessionary rates for young people in leisure facilities. Transport services, particularly in rural areas, should be improved.

## *Politics and youth policy*

■ Education for practical citizenship should be an important part of the school curriculum.

■ Politicians should find more effective, appropriate ways of communicating with young people.

■ Young people need the opportunity to participate directly in debate and decision-making over issues which matter to them.

■ Local forums for young people's participation should be supported and linked to formal consultation processes for local government and other public agencies.

■ The Scottish Parliament and Welsh and Northern Irish assemblies should develop regional and national youth forums.

■ Local MPs and decision-makers should have a role in developing more effective forms of involvement for young people, such as 'youth surgeries' and local 'youth cabinets'.

■ There should be a sustained focus on the coherence of the youth policy framework at national level and the development of local youth strategies. This means greater attention to the conjunction of education and employment policy issues with other policy areas: health, care, poverty, criminal justice, leisure and sport, community regeneration, family services. A Minister for Youth should be appointed, with primary responsibility for this coherence. This Minister should not be appointed without executive powers and administrative structures which accurately reflect the responsibility for coherence and coordination.

# Introduction

In the UK and across the developed world, the number of young people experiencing poverty, multiple disadvantage and social exclusion has become a major concern. A period of profound social, economic and cultural change has put increasing pressure on our assumptions about the nature of youth, and on the systems and structures that support young people to become healthy, independent and self-governing adults. Changes in media, consumer markets and popular culture have made images of youth more visible and more influential: the state of youth has become a barometer for wider social change and for the state of society as a whole. While many of the younger generation are thriving in the new environment, the marginalisation and disaffection of a significant proportion presents a serious challenge to government, public service providers, local communities and society.

One result of these changes is widespread public debate about the place of youth in society, the nature of adolescence, the responsibilities of parents, communities, the state and young people themselves. Another is the increasing priority placed on services for young people by governments. The clearest example of this is the way in which education has become a greater priority, both for government spending and for political debate. But many other policies and priorities reflect growing attention to the challenges faced by young people: employment, criminal justice, drugs, public safety, family services – the list goes on. In the UK, three out of five of Labour's early electoral pledges focused on children and young people. The centrepiece of the welfare to work programme, the New Deal for the young unemployed, aims to eradicate long-term unemployment among eighteen to 24 year olds. In Australia, Canada, the US and France, major public investments are being made in measures to reduce exclusion and disadvantage among young people.

One of the most striking features of this public debate has been the absence of young people's voices and, by and large, their lack of direct involvement in the policy process. Despite the growth in youth media, and alongside the wave of public concern about young people, there is growing recognition that their level of civic and political participation stands, in many countries, at a historical low point. In a recent MORI opinion poll, some 84 per cent of eighteen to 24 year olds said they did not trust politicians and some 70 per cent said they had never been consulted about their needs by politicians. The Real Deal is an attempt to address this situation: to give young people with experience of social exclusion the opportunity to put their views and to show how effective youth consultation contributes to inclusive politics and more effective policies.

For perhaps the first time, young people with direct experience of the most serious forms of exclusion and marginalisation have worked together to give their views on the issues and policies which affect them most. They have presented their views to policy-makers and politicians and produced a host of ideas and recommendations for making things better. This report sets out what they said.

## Social exclusion and disengagement

One starting point for public debate has been the widespread disengagement from formal political systems by young people. People under 25 are four times less likely to be registered to vote than any other age group. In 1995, only 6 per cent of sixteen to 34 year olds described themselves as 'very interested' in politics.[1] However, formal political involvement is a small part of the overall story.

The wider process of disengagement is partly a reflection of the fact that *forms* of political engagement are changing, and that younger people are more likely to be engaged in activities such as single issue campaigning and newer political causes which established political parties still struggle to adapt to. There is evidence that younger people are more likely than many assume to sign petitions, engage in voluntary activity and join certain kinds of political campaign. According to MORI, eighteen to 24 year olds are the group most likely to change their vote on the basis of a single issue. In order to engage fully with young people's concerns and motivations, government and political systems must change the way in which they consult and engage with them as well as encouraging their participation in elections. One reason for this problem is that there is no place for young people's opinions in the current system of government. Their participation is not systematically included in either policy formation or political campaigning.

Since the mid-1990s, a new policy theme has also gained momentum – how to address the systematic exclusion of large sections of the population by serious and multiple disadvantage. This disadvantage, spurred by the growth of poverty and the widening of income inequality in Britain and many other societies, has a direct and disproportionate impact on children and young people. The debate has also broadened to include cultural, social and geographical barriers to participation, brought together by the concept of *social exclusion*. This concept, while grounded in the analysis of poverty and material disadvantage, also emphasises the importance of the *dynamics* of exclusion: the processes by which it is deepened or alleviated and the interaction of different factors, such as work, family life, mobility and access to education, in producing different outcomes for individuals and communities. Tackling social exclusion is one of the fundamental challenges facing any society. It also connects directly to the debate over political and democratic engagement, since multiple deprivation and disadvantage are closely correlated with low levels of participation. One study of the younger generation in Britain found that people who are unemployed, from ethnic minorities or hold few educational qualifications are far less likely to see themselves as part of mainstream society and far less likely to vote or to make their views heard.[2] This point is confirmed by voting patterns more generally – in some of the most deprived inner city areas in the UK, voter turnout for local elections is less than 10 per cent. Rates of political participation (other than voting) are roughly twice as high among the middle class as among the working class. Those who may have most to gain from political change are least likely to be involved.

These problems have already spurred the creation of new ways to consult, involve and connect citizens with decisions which affect their lives. Campaigns to increase voter registration among the young and the development of new democratic forms such as citizens' juries, service user panels and consultative forums point to the determination of many, often voluntary, organisations to find innovative responses to these challenges.[3] Movements such as Local Agenda 21 and many other innovations in public service management have shown the potential of community-based consultation to involve citizens in identifying priorities, creating solutions and evaluating outcomes. In the UK, however, this work has been largely localised and often unrecognised. Good practice is seldom well understood, and most national policy is still made without the systematic involvement of those most affected by it.

The Real Deal project has addressed this situation with respect to young people and social exclusion. Its aim was to consult young people with real experience of disadvantage and exclusion on the issues that affected them and to find ways of presenting those views directly to policy and decision-makers. The project was organised through a partnership between

■ Save the Children, which works with local community organisations, including young people-led groups, to promote young people's rights and welfare
■ Centrepoint, a youth homelessness charity which helps newly homeless young people in greater London and works nationally with local groups to prevent youth homelessness
■ Demos, the independent think tank
■ Pilotlight, a small catalyst charity which initiated the project and works to highlight dispossession and encourage new approaches to social change
■ the Camelot Foundation, a charitable foundation providing financial support and partnership.

## How it worked

Ten groups of young people from around the UK were recruited through existing youth projects (see page 133, Methodology). In all, over a hundred young people were involved in the project. Each group, over a period of six to eight months, engaged in discussions and other activities designed around six core themes: leisure, work, education, community, transitions to adulthood, and government and decision-making. These were designed to cover a range of issues affecting young people's lives and of major policy questions, but framed to create flexibility for the young people themselves to focus on what mattered to them and to generate ideas and proposals which were independent of the detailed policy agenda set by government. Other issues such as family, crime and drugs also occupied much of the discussion time.

Young people from the project were also involved in a series of events and discussions with politicians and policy-makers during the course of the project. Real Deal fringe meetings were held at the Conservative and Labour Party conferences in 1998. In December 1998 a major policy seminar was held at 11 Downing Street and hosted by the Rt Hon Gordon Brown MP, Chancellor of the Exchequer. Young people presented their views and proposals and discussed them with people including the Prime Minister, the Secretary of State for Education and Employment, the Chief Secretary to the Treasury, other Ministers of State, senior officials from a range of government departments, and MPs with an interest in youth policy. This direct engagement was integral to the project and its outcomes have a bearing on this report. Other events were held by individual agencies to discuss aspects of the project and its relevance, for example, to the way young people are involved in the management of voluntary sector services.

Working in groups over a period of several months is a demanding job requiring a significant commitment from all involved. For young people experiencing the most severe forms of exclusion, for example rough sleeping, this form of sustained group work would have proved an unrealistic expectation. One of the difficulties of involving people who are effectively marginalised in the core decision-making processes of government and service providers is that their situation distances them from the 'threshold conditions' needed to engage in dialogue and exchange information: permanent addresses, regular routines of work, learning or leisure time, trust in professionals or in unfamiliar people. Added to this is the fact that the lives of many young people experiencing social exclusion are in constant flux. Rough sleeping, moving in and out of care, leaving or entering employment and training, and encounters with the criminal justice system are likely to take precedent over participation in a consultation project. As a result, 53 one to one interviews were conducted with homeless young people who were contacted through centres and cold weather shelters run by Centrepoint. The views and information that they offered are also presented in this report. They complement the views offered through the group work, offering a richer picture of the themes and issues, but it is important to remember that they were collected through one-off conversations and not through a more sustained process of consultation. Findings from these individual interviews are presented within the overall chapters on different themes, but are clearly marked as coming from a different source. Carrying out all aspects of this consultation project depended on the support structures and local bases already created by the work of the partner organisations.

It is important to note that, despite their participation in the same project and their discussion of common themes, there is considerable diversity in the backgrounds, experiences, ages and viewpoints of the young people represented in this report. Common themes emerge from what they say, as we will see. However, the recognition that, despite their experience of 'social exclusion', these young people have a wide range of perspectives is fundamentally important. The desire to be treated and respected as individuals is one of the primary themes to emerge, although many of the young people involved also felt a strong responsibility of representation for others who have not had the opportunity to put their views.

## The groups

There were two Centrepoint groups in London, one at Buffy House, a high-support hostel for young people with emotional difficulties and one at Camberwell Foyer. Camberwell is an 80-bed hostel for young people, which also provides employment and training services and acts as a New Deal gateway. The Camberwell group consisted of eight young people, between sixteen and 25, from different cultural backgrounds. The Buffy House group consisted of six people, many with mental health issues or high support needs. The group was mainly white British with equal numbers of men and women, aged between seventeen and 25. The eight remaining groups, as follow, were run in conjunction with Save the Children (SCF).

The Durham group was run by Save the Children. The group's members were aged between sixteen and 23. Some members of the group were care leavers and many were unemployed.

Tangents is a Scottish Voluntary Youth Organisation aimed at sixteen to 25 year olds. It is run by young people for young people and is based in central Edinburgh. Tangents uses peer education to promote young people's ideas and attitudes relating to the issues that affect them. The specific group for this project was formed through the national youth network and consisted of young people from both rural and urban areas of Scotland. There were seven females and four males aged between seventeen and 21. A number of the group were young parents, all of the group are or have been homeless. All are unemployed or working in a voluntary capacity. All have experience of drug use, either through taking drugs themselves, or their parents or friends taking drugs. The young people were keen to be involved in the project to promote their ideas, attitudes and life experiences.

The Aberdeenshire group was based in a small, rural community. The majority of the group were in their early twenties, though one participant was fourteen. They were recruited by their group worker who had had contact with them as individuals either as unemployed, homeless, single parents or as school pupils. After initial scepticism, attendance and participation in the sessions were high.

The SCF group in Oxford contained some young refugees who had come to the UK, mainly from Africa. Most of the refugees were living with foster parents in Oxfordshire.

The Belfast group took place on two Traveller camps, a few miles apart on the outskirts of Belfast. The initial sessions were conducted in June 1998 with a mixed group of young men and women. However, there were difficulties with this as young men and women in the Traveller community do not usually mix much at that age. So it was decided to split the group into men and women. One group consisted of five young women aged fourteen to sixteen and the other of three young men aged fifteen to twenty. In addition to the gender issues, the young people were unused to discussions and wary of research as the seeking of information about them was traditionally looked upon with suspicion. In addition, as there was a low level of literacy, the researchers had to be very oral in their approach. This issue was approached by using video in some cases and allowing the young people to interview each other. The young people were more at home discussing their community and attitudes to family than they were about subjects like education or leisure. The output from the group is focused around the subjects that were of interest, namely, community and work.

The Derry was drawn from young people who use Nucleus, a drug- and alcohol-free coffee bar and activity centre. Of the twelve young people who started the process, two had to drop out because of conflicting study and work commitments. The remaining ten comprised seven men and three women aged seventeen to 25. They all come from nationalist areas of Derry, which experience high rates of long-term and inter-generational unemployment and poverty. The majority of the group were early school leavers, although most have gone on to do do very well in informal or alternative education. Four work as peer educators, one is a single parent and one works in a local factory. Three of the group had been involved in another participation initiative, which explored their views on issues such as education and family.

The Hull group was based in the Rights and Participation Project (RAPP), a three-way joint agency between Hull Social Services, SCF and the Warren Resource Centre for Young People. The purpose of RAPP is to provide help, support and advice for vulnerable young people who are at risk. After the initial sessions, this group split into two smaller groups. Membership of one group was fairly fluid as some members were remanded during the project and others took their places. The other group, which consisted of four young men, had a stable membership.

The Cardiff group was based around the areas of St Mellons and Ely in Cardiff. Its members were somewhat younger than most other participants, around the fourteen to sixteen age group. It was run in conjunction with the Cardiff Youth Network.

## Attribution of quotes

Comments are not always attributed to individuals in the text that follows. Some participants in the conversations did not want to be identified, while others did. Where attribution might be incriminating, names have been changed or removed. Some quotations represent exchanges within groups; most are representative individual comments drawn from transcripts. In some cases, letters have been used to signify different participants in a discussion without revealing names.

## Structure of the report

**Who we are** covers issues of community, identity and family. This includes regional, national and ethnic identity, family, childhood and adulthood.

**How we live** covers lifestyle, leisure and recreation. It presents a picture of the young people's preferences and priorities in the things that they choose to do, and the very real constraints against which these choices operate.

**Learning and working** covers education, training and employment. It includes the young people's experiences of school, training and work, and their aspirations and ideas for improving the situation.

**What we need** covers experience of government services, and their views on the services and support that they feel would have helped. Specific views from the group consultation are brought out in earlier chapters and most of the material in this chapter comes from individual interviews.

**What we think** covers views of politics and politicians and ideas for improving the quality of political decision-making and the involvement of young people in it.

**Ideas for action** draws together the recommendations for policy and practice generated by the whole project. These include the results of workshops and debates as well as the core consultation and analysis of the findings.

Each chapter sets out the social and economic background, presents a cross-section of the young people's views and ends with a summary and conclusions.

The consultation produced rich sets of information in the form of transcripts, session records, specific ideas and proposals. Much of the fine detail applies to the specific local, national and regional contexts in which each group of young people lives. This is particularly important in relation to new political and administrative arrangements in Scotland, Wales and Northern Ireland.

# Who we are

## Community, identity and family

### Background

Amid widespread discussion of the nature and impact of change on contemporary society, one dimension stands out as the most complex, and perhaps the most confused. As the ways in which we work and communicate are transformed, as families and lifestyles change, and as new generations grow up, what constitutes our identity? Many of the structures which historically have bounded our sense of identity are undergoing profound adjustment. These range from the closest and most intimate – the family – through the spheres of economic life – social class, employer organisations – to the political and administrative – the nation state, the European Union. Alongside these structural changes are more fluid processes of cultural and value change. International research has shown the extent to which, across the world, fundamental values are shifting between the generations. Descended from a post-war generation which prioritised security, stability and material standards of living, younger people increasingly value freedom, self-expression and autonomy, alongside a host of ethical concerns which have emerged and strengthened over the past 30 years. The impact of consumer markets and the global media has created new connections between countries, lifestyles and cultures, enabling people to make far more choices, while bombarding them with new pressures and risks – the need to maintain the right brand identity, the fragility of technology-based relationships and the weakening of traditional communal ties.

For young people, these changes are especially important as they make the transition between stages of life, negotiating between the structures, values and assumptions that they have been brought up with and the ambitions, concerns and opportunities of their current experience. Many have more and more choices about where they live, how they live and with whom. They can experiment with different sorts of relationships and different sorts of employment. They can travel more and live in different countries, even, some claim, have greater social and class mobility. These freedoms present huge new opportunities, but also new risks and pressures which directly affect the majority of young people, a fact illustrated by the rise of depression and psycho-social disorders among the young.[4] For young people experiencing social exclusion however, many of these choices are not available, although the risks and pressures still exist, often magnified by disadvantage.

Alongside these basic challenges, a new political focus has developed during the 1990s, emphasising the importance of 'community' and the need to nurture forms of collective identity that offset and underpin the growth of individualism. Partly informed by 'communitarian' arguments,[5] there is also evidence that the population have become more concerned about quality of life and collective problems alongside more individualised concerns.[6] This change is reflected in the language and priorities of politics. Solidarity and mutual responsibility have become more explicit goals, and strong and active communities are held out as a way of achieving positive social outcomes without resorting to direct government intervention. Community is recognised as an essential support for people struggling against disadvantage.

But what does it mean in concrete terms? Is it realistic to appeal to notions of community which young people may no longer feel part of or want to join? How do we bring together the many different kinds of community that we can now belong to – occupational, local, international and lifestyle, to name just four?

This is why a clear understanding of the sources and limits of identity is so fundamental to effective consultation and successful policy. The challenge for government is to find ways of supporting its citizens as they try to reconcile the different strands of life that make up who they are. In the longer term, democratic systems should be capable of changing their governments to reflect the underlying aspirations and values of their members.

Nowhere are these issues more important than in understanding the family. It is well known that family structures have changed dramatically over the past 30 years. Divorce rates have increased dramatically: young people are more likely to be living in one-parent or step-families and more likely themselves to divorce. Between 1971 and 1990 in the UK, the number of young men divorcing between the age of twenty and 24 almost doubled from 3,529 to 6,740. The fact that the overall total is not greater is perhaps a reflection of the later age at which people of all social classes are getting married. In 1971, some 20 per cent of young men (aged sixteen to 24) and 35 per cent of young women were married. By 1991, this had fallen to 6 per cent and 13 per cent respectively.

Despite this decline in marriage, the UK still has the highest number of teenage mothers in the EU, with one in 32 women under twenty giving birth in 1992. With the age of first sexual activity also declining, almost 9,000 girls under sixteen became pregnant in 1996.

But the decline of marriage does not mean that people have stopped forming relationships. There has been a rise in cohabitation, both as a prelude to marriage and as a continuing relationship in which children are born. These patterns are strongly influenced by cultural factors, and census data shows that cohabitation among certain ethnic minority groups is relatively unusual.[7]

These and other changes are also having dramatic effects on the ways in which young people leave home. Both the traditional model of leaving home to marry and the newer trend of leaving to study at university are made more complex by a range of factors, including divorce and family conflict. The financial implications of parental divorce for children leaving home, with children particularly of 'first families' unable to rely on parental financial support, are the subject of increasing attention. Conflict with step-parents was, as we will see, frequently cited as a factor in the Real Deal discussions.

For those growing up in local authority care making the transition to adulthood is especially difficult. Care leavers are more at risk of social exclusion – unemployment, homelessness, lack of qualifications and long-term marginalisation. Care leavers move to independent living much earlier than most young people and often lack any form of continuing support, either financial or emotional. In addition, their transition to independent living can be brutally swift. Hence they have little chance to learn the life skills that children in families may be taught.[8]

The rise in youth homelessness is particularly important. Again, factors such as divorce (particularly conflict with step-parents) poverty and unemployment increase risk factors and, particularly for young women, physical and sexual abuse also contribute.[9] One piece of research found that as many as 40 per cent of young homeless women had been sexually abused.[10]

Finally, the influence of income and consumption patterns on identity cannot be overstated, particularly for young people in a world increasingly saturated by images of 'youth culture'. Young people are heavily targeted by advertising and consumer marketing, whether or not they have the means to spend. This change has been going on for most of the post-war period. High levels of employment and growing affluence from the 1950s to the late 1970s made this achievable for many, but the 1980s and 1990s have seen the transition to adult consumer become both more uncertain and more pressurised.

Rather than just being seen as a distinct market, youth cultural images are used in all markets and the so-called 'baby boomer' generation in particular have proved reluctant to shake off the 'youth' tag. On the positive side, youth subcultural identities and fashions (for example, rave culture) have tended towards the egalitarian and away from the class-based, at least in appearance. But while the opportunities for self-expression, enjoyment and diversion for some may be unequalled in previous generations, the gap between expectation and reality is wide for others.

As the population as a whole has become more affluent (in the 25 years from 1971 to 1996, real household disposable income almost doubled), income inequality has also widened. Where some 5 million people were officially classified as living in 'poverty' (income less than half the average) in 1979, the number is now nearer 13 million and close to one in three children are growing up in poverty.

Particular groups, such as disabled people, may face further disadvantage in terms of increased dependency upon carers and on low-paid jobs, which means they have less independent consumer power than other groups. In addition, while 'youth culture' (with the possible exception of the environmental movement) is often seen as an urban phenomenon, rural young people may suffer by comparison. Lack of rural transport, low pay and fewer leisure opportunities create specific disadvantages.

Above all, it is the growing power and influence of the media and the profile of 'youth culture' which seems to exert most influence and pressure to be 'seen to be having a good time'. Some evidence that this pressure is increasing and that a sense of dissatisfaction is widespread can be seen in an increase in the 'disorders of youth': eating disorders, substance abuse, depression and suicide.

Suicide among eighteen to 24 year olds doubled between 1974 and 1990 and is now the second commonest cause of death among young people.

# Findings

Over a series of meetings, the Real Deal explored how the young people involved viewed themselves and their communities. How did they feel about the communities they lived in, their families and their own identity? What influence did they have over the way they saw themselves and the way they were viewed by wider society?

The Real Deal participants expressed their identity in a many different ways and showed full awareness of the diverse influences on them. Overall, they were concerned that conventional or traditional ideas of community were not relevant to their lives. To some extent, their scepticism seemed to reflect a general sense of alienation from the mainstream. However, there was also a strong sense of wanting to belong and of the importance of mutual support and care. The fundamental influence of family life, in particular, emerged as a constant theme.

## *Community*

Overall, there was no strong consensus about what community is or whether it is a desirable thing. For most of the young people communities of choice, such as friends or colleagues, were as important as the community in which they lived. Few felt any strong sentimental attachment to the idea of community, although many, particularly those who have been homeless, are well aware of the dangers and risks of living in isolation, outside 'the community'.

A large proportion of the young people felt that their neighbourhoods (because of crime, drugs, unemployment and so on) did not 'qualify' as communities in any desirable sense. In other discussions the gap between ideal communities and reality was highlighted. The following discussion captures this ambivalence.

*In a small community, people do look like they are doing things together, but I don't think they are united. There seems to be something else going on.*

*Hypocrisy. Misfits. Keep to myself now.*

*I was born not far from where I live now. It's always been known as a really bad area.*

*Loads of drug dealers moved into my street and the whole area has gone down really badly.*

*I feel bad about not being able to bring this one [about-to-be-born child] around here, where it's safe to play outside. Going to the community bonfire and all that. I'd feel happier knowing it is at least safe around the streets around me. There are always kids playing in the street.*

*I don't think I'm part of the community where I live. I have friends in the gay community, the club scene, etc. I don't feel that I am part of any one community. My network of close friends are my community.*

*The weird thing about being an outsider in a community is that it feels like everything is going on somewhere else. (Edinburgh)*

Some young people expressed the view that while their communities were less than ideal, 'better' communities did exist, usually in more affluent areas.

*If you compare somewhere like ... to round here they've got all these good jobs, nice families and all the rest of it. Most of us are unemployed.*

*Look at ... compared to here. They all live in mansions ... got good parents around them, got jobs. (Cardiff)*

For many people, community meant their friends or other communities of choice, and existed on several levels.

*Everyone has three or four different communities – like work, social life and all. (Derry)*

Thus for many the notion of a community as the place where you are born and raised has little positive meaning. Greater mobility has contributed to this and many of the young people in the consultation had moved home several times, often large distances, while others were either new to the UK or had lived abroad.

For the Traveller group, however, the discussion about community was much more resonant. They define themselves as a separate community from 'settled people' and are very conscious of their identity as a minority group. Although, as one explained, within the Traveller community there are separate groups, usually based around family or camps.[11]

*I belong to the Irish Travellers first of all, but that is a very general thing. We do not have any connection at all with other travelling families except our own. We live on the Monagh, but we belong to one family there and we do not interfere with the others except that we get on well. (Belfast)*

This self-perception as an excluded minority community is reinforced by the fact that Traveller camps, although often near settled people, offer completely different physical conditions. One of the camps in this study only recently got a supply of water and electricity. Their young people's description was of a community under threat, in which the 'old ways' which had sustained them were dying and there was, as yet, little to replace them.

*If you see a good Travelling family there is nothing like it for good living and happiness. They are happy and feel proud of themselves. They have a love and understanding of nature and the earth and we have a language that is good. But the strange thing here is that young people do not want the language any more. You could sit in the trailer and listen to your parents talk and you wouldn't have a clue what they are saying about you. Even you will find that some of them will laugh at the mention of the language and they will mock you if they hear you talk it. That is sad. They call you an "antague manin", which is an old-fashioned person.*

*Sometimes what I would really like to do is go way for a few days and camp out in the country and live under the sky. We could teach the young people to cook on the fire and learn the old ways about survival and such. It would be a good idea for kids to learn that stuff and it would help the teenagers to have more understanding of their own ways. It would be good to have something like that in the summertime, but I can't see how people will want to leave their houses again. The ways are changing fast.* **(Belfast)**

This sense of pride and history was noticeably absent from many other groups' discussions. The significance of loss of community was made clearer in the discussion on exclusion.

## Communities and exclusion

The exploration of positive and negative images of community threw light on the young people's perceptions of inclusion and exclusion.

Negative images revolved around the notions of communities as 'interfering':

*I think community is a whole load of people who nose into your private life. If you have tattoos and are a single parent they judge you. I don't feel a part of the community. I've lived in a few places in my time and I can't settle down and put roots to a community because of the hassle and the stigma that follow you.* **Mandy (Durham)**

For a smaller number of young people, there was a positive side to the closeness of communities. This seemed to reflect a recognition that the other side of 'interfering' can be support and security.

*They [communities] are as oppressive as relationships are, but living without relationships is difficult. Communities have their bad sides but they also have lots of positive sides to them. It varies from community to community, but saying they shouldn't exist is just saying that everyone should be out for themselves and completely isolated.* **Tigger (Oxford)**

*The area where I live everybody knows everybody and they know my dad as a strict man, number of his car, they could tell his life history if they want to, known as a no-nonsense man, a reputation, so there was that respect there. It's kind of a confined neighbourhood like if something bad happens, everybody helps but the interaction has a limit, people still do that between themselves but us as a family, we don't.* **(Camberwell)**

Those individuals who felt that communities were about prying into your business felt the way to avoid this was to 'keep yourself to yourself'. There was also the suspicion that communities could 'turn on you' – suddenly excluding you when you felt you were secure.

> *Your neighbour can seem to be very, very friendly and then they can turn on you.*
> *(Camberwell)*

Exclusion from the community was a topic that came up in most groups and in several guises. For some, it was simply about personal feelings of isolation, often provoked by lack of support from family.

> *My dad always goes out, no one's ever in the house for me ... I'm sat there, and then I*
> *go to work and I'm boxed in the little room ... what community have I got? (Cardiff)*

More particularly, specific forms of exclusion were highlighted. These included racism, stereotyping by appearance or age and by neighbourhood.

School is often identified as the place where these feelings of exclusion start, as two young people from the Edinburgh group discussed.

> *I was ostracised at school because I didn't wear a school uniform. I had my nose pierced*
> *and never really fitted in.*

> *I couldn't fit in at school because of my English accent. I had lived in England for years*
> *and when I came back I wasn't accepted because of my accent. (Edinburgh)*

Racism was discussed in several groups. Comparisons were sometimes made between where the young people were currently living and communities they felt to be more tolerant.

> *When I moved here [Oxford] I asked someone where is the town – they would direct me*
> *backwards. In London black men want to talk to you, whereas in Oxford they will ask*
> *you where you're from. In Hackney people help more. Rudy (Oxford)*

> *If I go out in Newcastle or Durham – this isn't me being racist – you never see many*
> *black people or Asians or Indians. In Leicester everyone mixes together like one big happy*
> *family. Here, if three or four Asian people walked in together they would get brayed. Zoe*
> *(Durham)*

The idea that community was more fragmented than in the past was raised by some. A few argued that communities used to be closer and people were less afraid to speak to one another in their parents' generation. Others felt that some of the tension in their community came from inter-generational conflict and that they were more open-minded that previous generations.

*I'd say against us there's more conflict off older people – mid-forties, fifties. You stand on the streets, they just think you're up to trouble because you're young, boys in baseball caps, things, whatever, the way you're dressed.*

*People our age are more open ... to other races ... more of an open mind than our parents. And you've got adults teaching, no wonder why kids are coming home from school each day crying "I got called a black bitch today" ... in school it's the way of the parents, it's the older generation.* **(Cardiff)**

Given their ambivalence about the desirability of community and their own feelings of exclusion, there was a surprising degree of consensus when the groups were discussing the notion of who did not belong in their community. Criminals, prostitutes and drug pushers were all named, as were policemen, security guards and beggars. The Hull group's suggestion of who should be 'out' of the community included 'smackheads, coppers, security guards and prozzies.'

*Do you know what I think should be out? Smackheads who have got, you know, bairns. Bairns looking like tramps, all they [parents] care about is their smack habit.* **Budgie (Hull)**

Some young people recognised that, as some of them were drug users and had been in trouble with the law themselves, there was a possibility that this would be seen as inconsistent.

*Interviewer: Is the beggars a bad thing?*
*Dunny: Yeah.*
*Emily: You begged yourself.*
*Dunny: Ages ago.* **(Hull)**

Nevertheless, the notion of crime as a threat to communities came through quite strongly.

*Criminals. No one wants criminals as part of their community so they aren't going to accept them.* **Tanya (Durham)**

## Communities and power

Although seen by many as undesirable, criminals, especially drug dealers, were widely regarded as having power in the community.

*Drug dealers have power over the community.* **Christine (Durham)**

*They can get you addicted to drugs ... they say ... oh you can pay so much for this ... and you would.* **(Hull)**

*In our place it took the drug dealers to come down and sort this problem out with this
one wee guy in his shop and the ice cream van. Nobody else would get involved.*
**(Edinburgh)**

Parents, social workers (though not teachers) and the police were all credited with having power in
the community by some young people. But there was very little consensus about power and little
that tied the notion of power in the community to a wider context such as government. Some young
people in the Derry group argued that Sinn Fein politicians had power in their community, but that
derived from their role in 'policing' rather than their political power. Some maintained that they
had power over their own lives, though a more typical view was that there are 'those above us, with
more power than us'.

*What are we supposed to do? There's the sickheads and there's the old fucking fogies and
they won't listen because they don't think we've got power, cos we're younger.* **(Cardiff)**

Several seemed resigned to the fact that crime in their own community affected people like themselves, 'they're robbing from the poor'. Other felt that ethical distinctions between crime against
houses and crimes against businesses should be observed,

*R: In the circle of people, I used to do things with, you didn't do people's houses, you did
businesses … because of the …*
*Interviewer: The insurance?*
*R: The insurance, and because they could afford it and of course you go wildly off trying
to justify yourself but people who own these businesses … and if you was to leave them
alone you end up like a shabby old man, like an alcoholic, they wouldn't spit on you on
the street, though … So why should you do anything for them? So that's the way people
rationalise it to themselves.* **(Aberdeenshire)**

## One to one findings

### Community

The young people who took part in one to one interviews strongly echoed the themes raised by the
consultation groups. Community was an idea that many found difficult to relate to. Several asked
'what do you mean by community?' Some vehemently rejected the whole notion.

*No, I don't [feel part of a community]. No, I fought it at home to make it in this world.
You have got to make it for yourself. There is no community willing to help you or are
helping you at the moment – not that they can't, there are the resources there to help you
if want to but they don't.* **Tim, Black, 24, London**

Community was widely understood in terms of location and belonging. For many, the image of a
close-knit local community had little resonance, as they had moved about frequently or no longer
lived in the area they were most familiar with. One person pointed out that he did not feel part of

a community as he had not 'been here long enough to feel like that'. When asked about when he did feel part of a community, he replied:

> *Manchester, which is a very, very small city and everybody knows everybody and because I didn't have any enemies I didn't have anybody to worry about anything, I used to walk around without any problems and so did feel part of the community.*
> **Marcus, White, 20, London**

Linked to this was an understanding of community as people who had known each other for a long time.

> *Neighbours. Buddy buddies for years. That's the community when people have known each other for years. I mean I go to the pub on a certain day, have a gin and that's the community.* **David, White British, 24, London**

Many of the young people also had strong views of the way local communities treated 'outsiders'. One argued that rural courts treated people from outside cities more severely than the local residents. Not belonging to such a certain area, however, was not perceived to be negative in itself. One young woman who claimed no desire to be part of a community explained:

> *To me just places where you've lived for a long time or where you feel you belong and things like that [are communities]. I don't think I belong anywhere, but I suppose you can belong somewhere if you want to, so I suppose I don't particularly want to belong anywhere. Quite happy roaming around by myself.* **Magenta, Black British, 22, London**

For the majority, community as location was felt to be limiting, and often not a viable option. Some felt it was important to feel a sense of community in their current circumstances.

> *It depends, community is lots of different things, you want a community when you're living in a hostel atmosphere like a group of people who are in like the same situation as yourself and things like that. I mean community could be anything, like in Liverpool where I'm from, the community could be something like the little house where I come from.* **Stacey, White, 18, London**

The version of community which had more resonance was based on people and circumstances. As one person explained:

> *It's being part of a large group, in fact more than a group, but getting along well with them and them getting along well with you, basically it's the same as having a large group of friends.* **Marcus, White, 20, London**

*People that want to involve themselves with other people and find out what other people are like, what people are doing, not being nosey but like, but caring, sort of thing, which I think is good.* **Mike, Maltese, 23, London**

One ideal to emerge from the interviews was of a community who helped and talked to one another. Some said that, although most of the time they felt they did not belong to a particular community, in instances where they had received help and support they had felt a sense of community.

*Sometimes I do [feel part of a community] but sometimes I tend to single myself out but at times like this when people like Centrepoint help you, you think there it is, that's all a community, like a family all together and that I'm proud to live in a place like this where everyone helps everyone.* **Janette, Afro-Caribbean, 18, London**

But even this definition had its problems. Some pointed to an oppressive side of community in which, by being part of a community, there was a pressure to conform to certain standards and be a 'sheep'. The most obvious expression was people wearing the same clothes, but it also extended to the way people behave.

*I suppose being a woman and stuff [is something I feel a part of] but I'm not really into girl power and all that. But I don't know, community for me is not something I really want to belong to anyway, because there are so many rules and you have to do many things. There are bonuses obviously but seems like too much hassle. If you're just by yourself you can do what you want, don't have to answer to anyone, can do it your way, full stop.* **Magenta, Black British, 22, London**

Another factor affecting young people's ability to identify with community was the tendency and need to be moving around. Many stressed the importance of self-reliance and argued that their community was the homeless community.

As in the group consultation, the young people's disassociation with the popular notion of a local or wider community suggests a strong feeling of isolation and exclusion. One person commented that they would be part of a community when they had a home. Another argued that the older generation excluded young people.

Conversely, there was a very strong sense of identity with a 'homeless community'. Some said they had only felt really part of a community since 'living on the streets'. This community was variously described, for some it was 'people who look out for each other and people you can talk about stuff and understand them', and less positively it was 'the people in this hostel, the drug dealers outside, the stingers (people dependent on drug dealers) and the beggars outside'. One young woman described other sex workers as part of her community due to a 'certain sharing of experience'.

*You know, there is a community feel there [on the streets]. It's like I can come along tonight and not know any of the people here [in the hostel] but because we shelled out and we know what it's like to be at the bottom of the heap, then there is a bond in there and they're the last people who are going to turn round and stitch you up a lot of the time. Sometimes things happens but, for the most part, you become united in that. ... I mean most of the outside world is ... a world full of strangers. I guess in many respects when you end up on the street, you have to.* **Paul, Irish-English, 24, London**

# Perceptions and images of young people

## One to one findings

The young people involved in one to one interviews had strong and clear views about the way they were perceived. Often this was expressed in views on other people's attitudes to homelessness. This was strongly connected, however, to wider misunderstanding of young people in general. Few identified with any media representation of young people and many felt that the media was manipulative. For example, one young woman had been approached by a television researcher working on a drama series about prostitution. The woman refused to help, as she felt that the researcher was exploiting her situation for the sake of a television programme. Another person, who had participated in a documentary about homelessness, found that her portrayal did not capture the way she really felt. Some were more positive, explaining that the media could play a role in alerting people to homelessness and could help people.

Many felt that the media concentrates on negative portrayals of young people, focusing on crime and drugs. This was considered unjust and inaccurate, as 'nothing like us or not what I've seen of young people anyway'. 'Doing horrendous things' was felt to be something a minority of young people did.

> *Exaggeration, that sort of thing ... like the local newspaper where I'm from, it's all youths this and youths that and that's what they think of youth, kind of like, to rob them, like taking heroin, and the like.* **Bill, Scottish, 20, London**

Understandings of how the public (commonly understood to be adults) viewed young people was equally negative. Young people, it was felt, were viewed as 'tearaways' and 'criminals'. Perceptions of homeless young people were far worse. Many said the public saw homeless people as 'worthless', 'invisible', 'no hopers' and 'criminals'. Generally people felt the public 'looked down' on homeless young people, preferring to ignore them. A common view was that wealthier people tended to be even less interested in helping homeless young people. Despite these negative perceptions, some also said that there were some people who showed genuine concern; some had experiences of people giving them phone numbers should they need any help.

> *If they're homeless, they get looked upon with a great amount of disrespect. If they are young they are classed as reckless troublemakers.* **Gavin, European, 24, Devon**

> *The people who've probably got the most to spare are the tightest about it, and you have ... Some people treat you with disdain and that's horrible. Some people look at you – well they look through you as though you're invisible.* **Paul, Irish-English, 24, London**

Some felt that the public somehow blamed them for their situation. One explanation put forward for hostile public attitudes towards homeless young people was that their presence on the street called into question values such as family which should have prevented homelessness.

> *I think that the older public kind of view us as the cause of this problem and that problem, you know, it's this or us, which I don't completely disagree with but I don't completely agree with either because I don't think that one whole generation can be to blame for the whole world's problems. All of us really don't have that much power to do half of the things that we're being accused of, and I think the youth really is misunderstood. It sounds like an easy way out but I think that we're really misunderstood.* **Lydia, Afro-Caribbean, 23, London**

> *I think people see homeless young people in a completely different way to normal young people because they're the ones who have done something bad. Otherwise they wouldn't have been kicked out, and we've got to have, because it brings into question the whole system of families and everything else.* **Ruby, White European, 20, London**

> *Crime – it's always a young person; drugs – it's always a young person; or the young mothers who get pregnant all the time. So it's always young people. Basically everybody blames young people.* **Neil, Irish, 19**

Black young people also talked about racial stereotyping, arguing that it was often assumed that black people were often thought of as 'crooks' and 'drug dealers'. Another argued that wider perceptions of black people limited people's aspirations.

> *I just feel as though within society that I'm stereotyped anyway and when I do go out into the public I find it harder for myself just in general having to prove myself, whether it be work, education, a skill of any sort. I just feel as though me as a young black woman we're either good for singing or a sport and that's what makes young black people tend turn to anyway from climbing up that corporate ladder.* **Suzanne, Afro-Caribbean, 20, London**

Others found it difficult to generalise about public perceptions, arguing that attitudes depended on the person and also the look of the young person. Dress was especially important. Smarter clothes, it was argued, were considered to be 'all right', whereas 'scruffy' clothes labelled the young person as 'underneath' society.

> *I prefer to wear [suits], you know I do enjoy showing how intelligent I am, because of the stereotype of the youth not being very clever, always wanting to steal, always wanting to commit crime, I'm the total opposite of the stereotype.* **Marcus, White, 20, London**

> *What I say is this, the thing is, all right I can dress smart, I really do. No, I'm not a hypocrite. I can be walking along the road and a young or middle-aged woman, a young woman like yourself could be walking towards me and all right I'll look, just to see who*

*it is like, and I can feel them grabbing their bags and I am getting tired of it. Tell her a bit that she's wrong. I know that she's doing it because she's seen me – a white puffa jacket … and I think to myself, she thinks that I'm going to rob her. It's so unfair, when I don't know them. I've never robbed anyone in my life.* **Mike, Maltese, 23, London**

# Identity

## Findings

In the group discussions of identity there was also a general feeling that people were judged too much on how they looked. This could refer to the fact that they did not have the latest 'name' labels and were made to feel inadequate, or the fact that they were young, wore baseball caps or other symbols of youth, and so were judged to be criminals. Often this was associated with the area or neighbourhood that you come from.

*When you go up to the centre, innit – if we meet someone from Splott, we're from St Mellons – so you're a slapper, are you … just because you live in one place they brand you … a policeman says, "So where are you girls from?" because we were just talking to him, so he says, "And how much trouble have you been in?"* **(Cardiff)**

Changing forms of national and regional identity were also important to many of the young people. For some this was a source of pride. This was particularly the case in Scotland.

*You can get away with being Scottish and loud but not if you're English.*

*At this international youth festival in Cuba, we had to march and the English refused to march under an English flag and no one wanted to march under the Union Jack, so everyone marched under the saltire and the response we got was amazing. Everyone just assumed that all of us were Scottish. Everyone from other countries knew something about Scotland and about our struggle for independence.*

*What makes Scotland stronger is that we have a national identity and the English just seem to live off of everyone else's.* **(Edinburgh)**

*I would never call myself British, cos they just regard you as English. I remember one time the Lockerbie thing, on CNN, Sky telly it was an aircraft in England. I didn't know Lockerbie was a borough of London like. See like in Europe, especially pubs in Amsterdam or Belgium or Paris, they will take Scottish money off you, if you haven't got francs, but they won't take English money off you. No chance like.* **(Aberdeenshire)**

In Derry, despite being from the nationalist community, the young people expressed a sense of connection to both the Republic and the UK.

*I feel comfortable in the South. While I'm not a republican, I think it is one Ireland.*

*I'd move to Galway tomorrow. I've had the situation where my family had to live there because of the Troubles.*

*I live in the UK and Northern Ireland. If I had a choice between London and the South, I'd pick London.*

*I don't mind connecting with Britain. It's the closest land mass to here. It's good for a holiday. It's different. I like how cosmopolitan it is. Religion isn't a problem there, maybe skin colour is instead.*

For the Derry group, religion, even for those who were not believers, played a large part in their sense of identity.

*Whether you live in Creggan or Culmore, you're still part of the Catholic community.*

A couple of young people in the Oxford group were also Christians and church was seen as very influential in their lives and sense of identity.

*The church has been a great impact on my life – it's really changed my life.* **Billy (Oxford)**

More surprisingly, its role in the community was raised by several young people, even those who were not religious.

*Penfold: Put vicars in. They help everyone out.*
*Interviewer: How?*
*Penfold: Just to get something to eat and some money and that.*
*Budgie: The woman in the church as well. Every time we go there she gives us something.* **(Hull)**

*Yeah, that [the church] is a community. I wouldn't say it was mine, but it is still a community.* **R (Aberdeenshire)**

Others were less convinced.

*[There] used to be a charismatic community group at the church and everyone had to go. Used to come and hassle you on the streets if you didn't come. Hypocrisy. All these people pretending to be good Christians and then going home and kicking shit out their dog and that.* **(Edinburgh)**

To explore the idea of local identity further the young people were asked how they would feel if they had to move. For many, especially those who were refugees or had been homeless or had simply moved around a lot as children, the idea of moving was not problematic. But in groups whose members were part of more settled communities, people expressed concerns about relocation.

*I wouldn't want to move out of the area. Because it's different and they would call you a Macam or a Geordie. When I was down London they turned around and said, oh you're Macams, the first thing they said. I'm proud of where I'm from but I don't think it should be the first thing someone classes you as.* **John (Durham)**

Other were concerned about how outsiders saw their neighbourhoods.

**Hoysey:** *We don't want people to see that [boarded up shops] when they come to Hull*
**Dunny:** *It makes the city look a public disgrace.* **(Hull)**

The Cardiff group complained strongly that visitors were being shown a false picture of their city, with resources being concentrated on the Cardiff Bay development at the expense of areas like St Mellons or Splott.

The widely varying experiences of Real Deal participants make it difficult to generalise about the young people's regional or national sense of identity. Those in Scotland certainly seemed to feel a greater sense of national identity than others. The Derry group, despite being all from Catholic nationalist backgrounds, felt comfortable with the notion of some connection with Britain, despite seeing themselves as Irish. The group workers felt that this finding was unlikely to be replicated among older generations.

## Identity and adulthood

There was no clear picture among the groups of 'being an adult' and what it entails. A strong sense emerged from the discussions that the different elements of becoming an adult did not fit together for them in any straightforward way. Many of the young people expressed the view that legal adulthood (being able to vote, get married or whatever) was out of step with emotional or psychological feelings of maturity. They pointed out that events previously associated with adulthood, such as sexual relationships or parenting, in fact happened to people as young as thirteen, but were not necessarily accompanied by feelings of adulthood.

There was general agreement that being an adult was a state of mind rather than a legal definition and it was often, though not always, associated with independence or responsibility. Many of the young people did not regard being an adult as being empowered to make their own decisions. Whether this is because their childhoods have been freer of the kind of constraints imposed on earlier generations (staying out late, drinking, sex) or simply a reflection of their uncertainty about the adult world is unclear. Many have also had experience of taking major responsibility, either for themselves or for others, earlier than most. But as one young person in the Edinburgh group put it rather bleakly:

*I think when you turn fifteen that's when you realise how shit the world actually is. Fucking hell, no one is really gonna take an interest and help me.*

For most, the forms of adulthood, such as work or independent accommodation, were not seen as necessarily conferring adult status. The range of ages at which different adult rights were conferred added to this confusion.

Some felt they were more mature than their years suggested, while others had taken on adult responsibilities, either caring for their parents or for siblings. Others, such as the refugees, had been forced to leave home very young. As one young man in Edinburgh explained,

> *At home I was the parents to my mum, because she's got all sort of weird illnesses. I was always the parents, so I think I've always been in control.*

Despite these responsibilities, many knew they did not feel like adults.

> **Smithy:** *You know if you have someone die in your family, say it's your mum, and the girl in the family, does she have to be more adult because her mum's died, take a lead role? It doesn't make you more of an adult it just means you're using your common sense.*
> **Christine:** *What it makes you do is grow up faster.*
> **Smithy:** *It doesn't make you an adult though, cos you're the same age.*
> **Marzy:** *Yeah, but you're classed as adult if you're handling loads of responsibility*
> **Smithy:** *Yeah, but you might not be.*
> **Marzy:** *Well yeah, but if you are handling it in an adult way, you might not be legally adult but you can still act adult.* **(Durham)**

> *I was attending college and had a part-time job at age fifteen or sixteen. While I was in college, between lessons, I would do extra hours. Also, looking after my mum, adulthood came early, looking after my mum since the age of eight. Between the ages of eight and seventeen, still a child but with adult responsibility, mixture of both.* **Emma (Buffy House)**

Most agreed with this view that being an adult was about feeling an adult rather than being a particular age. Though some young people took a rather more prescriptive view.

> *I don't know if this is anyone else's opinion, but if you're 25 and you still haven't got your life sorted out, there must be something wrong with you.* **Hoysey (Hull)**

For a minority, being an adult was connected with notions of 'outgrowing' types of behaviour such as drugs or crime.

> **Stu:** *If I could change, to do better things, better activities, then I would.*
> **D:** *I don't want to be a fucking druggie, a low life all the time.*
> **Stu:** *But if we didn't like it we wouldn't do it.*
> **Interviewer:** *So how do you think you might change that, D?*
> **D:** *We're only young now.*

*Interviewer: So you think you'll change? In a few years ... or ...?*
*D: I'll grow out of it.*
*Interviewer: How are you going to grow out of it?*
*D: Get a job, settle down, get a bird. Get your head together and that, isn't it?*
*Interviewer: How do you do that though? Do you do it as you grow up or do you just decide it's good to do?*
*Budgie: You just decide, you do it if you have a bird.*
*Penfold: You do it as you grow up, you're changing.*
*Stu: Yeah, but if you find a bird who takes drugs then you're fucked, aren't you?*
*Interviewer: So you see women as a way of helping you settle down and get off drugs?*
*Budgie/Stu/D: Yeah. (Hull)*

Other views of adulthood were suggested by some, but there was no widespread agreement that any of these states were synonymous with adulthood.

One young person saw making your own decisions as a key part of adulthood.

*I think maybe for me, being an adult is basically about making decisions without the opposition or disapproval of parents. Such as you can choose who your partner is without them trying to stop that, you can do the job you want without others' disapproval. Whatever.* **Chris (Buffy House)**

Whereas for another it was about independent living.

*I suppose the transition is really learning to live on by yourself within the system, taking from it what you need. That was all when I was seventeen, about two years ago. I've always just got myself sorted with work and I've never got myself into situations that have been too difficult to get out of. (Edinburgh)*

Others thought it was about being taken seriously by the adult world.

*When you are about 30 or something and people start listening to you. Nobody listens to you when you are younger.* **Lisa**

*Older people can get away with making an arse of themselves but when you're like our age they say look at that kid.* **John (both Durham)**

Only in the Traveller community was attaining adulthood still seen as a distinct, age-related phenomenon. Travellers tend to marry young and adolescence is a short period, approximately thirteen to sixteen. The transitions appear to be different and perhaps more difficult for boys than for girls.

*If you leave school at the age of eleven or twelve or at the time of your confirmation, whichever comes first. Then you are expected to start acting like a man. This is symbol-*

*ised by the fact that a boy will begin to ride a bike about the age of twelve. He is seen to be no longer a child, but he is scorned if he is still on a bike at the age of fourteen. Then he is expected to be able to drive a van or lorry and he is expected to be able to help with the work and be productive.* **Young man (Belfast)**

The notion of adulthood was undoubtedly fluid and sometimes confusing one for most of the young people in the Real Deal consultation. What is striking is the lack of enthusiasm many displayed towards the notions of adulthood. Rather than being about freedom from parental control, empowerment and the chance to express oneself fully, many regarded it as about responsibility and a narrowing, rather than an opening up, of choices. This seems partly to be a reflection of the fact that for many, despite prevailing public and media conceptions of young people, they had significant experience of taking responsibility in the face of different challenges and hardships. There was also a strong sense that consistent, appropriate support in making the transition to adulthood was hard to find.

## Class as a source of identity

The discussion of class seemed to reflect wider debates about its changing structure and importance. Some of the young people were resistant to the idea of 'class', while other felt it was a bit irrelevant or old-fashioned. But nonetheless, the belief that 'it all comes down to money' and that they were discriminated against in economic and social terms remains powerful. Some felt that they were 'looked down upon':

*X: Like when I got caught taking Parker pens out of people's school bags, I had about fifteen different ones in my bag, yeah, and they caught me and I just lied and said I was kicking the bag around and a pencil case fell out of it and I got away with it!*
*Y: That's appalling. You should have come to my school.*
*X: Yeah, that's because my school was nice and posh and they don't believe you can do anything like that.* **(Buffy House)**

*Well the posh people don't mix with the ruffians. We're not ruffians but that's what they think ... they think they're better than anyone else.* **(Cardiff)**

Although there was no clear notion of 'class solidarity', the young people viewed themselves as different from 'posh people'.

*Interviewer (during discussion about drugs): Penfold lives in a posh area and he's a smackhead.*
*Penfold: I don't live in a posh area, my dad does.*
*Stu: You live there.*
*Penfold: No, I don't ... My dad's only just moved to there! I don't live there, how am I middle class?*
*Emily: We aren't saying you are middle class.*
*Penfold: Yes, he fucking is.*

*Emily: It's just that you live in a middle-class area, which you do.*
*Interviewer: Penfold, seriously, is being called middle class a real insult to you?*
*Penfold: Yes.* **(Hull)**

Few young people made explicit connection between class and politics, though as this discussion from the Cardiff group makes clear, there was a feeling that the young people understood about 'real life' because of their backgrounds.

> *And because we have grown up on an estate where there is like teenage mothers and drugs and things like that we are more aware of what politics are about.*

> *Like some of them [politicians] might be middle class as they were growing up, or upper class or something like that. I don't know if there are any politicians which are working class, but if they were, then they realise the issues, which is a better thing.*

Many argued that power was exercised from above and not by people like themselves.

> *That's why they need us to give men in suits ... they've got the money, haven't they? You wouldn't see an MP living in St Mellons or Splott .* **(Cardiff)**

> *Yeah, cos you wouldn't have someone who had been on the dole all their life suddenly become health minister.* **Zoe (Durham)**

> *X: At the end of the day how hard have politicians had their life?*
> *Y: Do they understand where we are coming from?*
> *Z: Because they haven't experienced it.*
> *X: They haven't got many ideas about what it is like.*
> *Y: Don't know what's going on with our generation.*
> *X: Yeah, but our class we are just a statistic but like with upper classes what they say matters with all the politicians, they are higher up in class so what they vote for counts, more closer to them.* **(Cardiff)**

## Identity and consumption

For Real Deal participants discussion about money tended to focus on budgeting for the basics rather than acquiring the trappings of consumerism. Budgeting had proved difficult for many young people living independently for the first time and many reported getting into debt. Their views of money were more concerned with the need to provide themselves with basic living needs rather than luxuries. Though some did report pressure to wear 'designer' clothes, others either felt themselves immune to this or were more realistic about their ability to participate in that culture.

> *Then I got my own flat and a job paying £250 per week doing night shift. I still couldn't pay the bills. I still haven't learnt how to budget.* **(Edinburgh)**

*Marzy: I don't give a shit, I don't care what anyone thinks about what I wear.*
*Lisa: But some people do.*
*Marzy: Yeah, it is for a hell of a lot of people.*
*John: I think people who really need those label clothes are really insecure.*
*Christine: It depends on the social circles you are in doesn't it, really. If all your friends are wearing designer labels then you'll want them.* **(Durham)**

The fashion industry and pressure on people to confirm to a certain appearance came in for some criticism and was seen as exclusionary.

*But if you go into places like Para and the Mini or in town or anything, you know like that clubbie bar, then you'll get the nobby folk that are looking down on you and like "What the hell are you doing here? That's not a label top you're wearing."*
**(Aberdeenshire)**

Others recognised the pressures that the gap between expectation and reality could cause.

*Everything's more appealing now, faster cars and that, and the young'uns do not get nay money, but there's better stuff like computers so there's more burglaries and car crime.*
**Big Dunc (Durham)**

Some argued that, while they may be able to resist such pressures for themselves, they would be unable to do so for their children.

*I fall into the pressure all the time. I've got two children. I can point out and agree with exactly what you're saying, eh, "labels, labels, labels", but I'll do exactly the same thing. Like I said to you, I'll go into the Gap and buy my kids clothes. I don't want my kid going to school with not very nice clothes, because I know from my own experience … it's not nice. You send your kids with not nice clothes, then he's gonna get a hard time.*
**(Cardiff)**

The pressure on parents to ensure that their children had the 'right' clothes was well understood, though there was some debate in the Cardiff group about the correct priorities for parents.

*X: Look at my mother … she wants me to go to university and that she won't be able to afford it, yet she spends £80 on having my hair straightened.*
*Y: When my mother and father lived up in Pentwin – I always had this argument with my mother and father and it's a great example – because my mother and father bought us everything when we were young. But then as soon as we got to our teenage years, we had nothing because most of the time they didn't save any money. They had no money to send us to college, no money to give us like a nice eighteenth birthday present, no money to help us on our way when we shared a flat, no money for anything. But then the women next door, who used to live next to us, give her kids nothing throughout the years. No decent Christmas presents, no decent clothes, but both of them – one's a scientist and*

*one's a lawyer in London – and they've got everything. And I have this argument with my parents, that if you gave me less when I was younger, you could have given me more which would have meant more for my future.*
*Z: But how would you have felt when you were younger?*
*Y: I don't know …*
*Z: We're not exactly completely mature are we? So we aren't going to turn round and say, no mum, I don't want that money, put it away for when I goes to university, you don't, do you?*

## One to one findings

The common theme of alienation from wider society resonated throughout the discussion of identity in one to one interviews. The young people talked about others in society, including other young people, and emphasised their differences, from dress to opportunities and attitudes.

> *Young people, there are so many sorts of young people, starting from the social level, people who have got money, go to universities, wear nice clothes, these are from the people opposite of those round the corner selling drugs or doing prostitution … young people that are already on the street.* **Fabio, Black Italian, 24, London**

Some said that they had always felt this sense of difference. One young man talked about being 'just me, a rebel without a cause' when younger, something he now regretted ('It was what I believed in, but it was a load of rubbish'). Others felt that it reflected other people's judgement and misunderstanding of them and their circumstances.

> *You see yesterday I was walking down the street with bloody no shoes on my feet, they assume that I was mad. Start sort of screwing up for no reason, people say you're mad, it's like at school you know when I used to dance and that, they used to say,"Oh, he's mad."* **Simon, Black British, 21, London**

Others had positively rejected an identification with 'most other people'. For example, one young man talked about his identification with Buddhism as a rejection of materialism, arguing, 'Most of us don't have that [material goods]! But you have to teach people to not be attached to them.'

Most held a very strong sense of self-identity. Their experiences, even bad ones, were felt to have created their identity. This was far from negative: young people spoke confidently of not wishing to change any of their experiences, since they contributed to 'making me who I am and what I am.'

> *I wouldn't change anything, I've now become a stronger young woman, and had experience. Hopefully it will help me throughout my career, or better someone else. I wouldn't change anything.* **Suzanne, Afro-Caribbean, 20, London**

> *Everything makes you what you are so you need everything to be the person that you are. If you take away something then you won't have that same experience and that same*

*knowledge, so you have to have everything that happens to you whether it's good or bad as you learn from everything, whether you want to or not. You might make the same mistake again but you learn something from it the second time than from when it happened the first time. So I wouldn't change anything about myself or what's happened.*
**Magenta, Black British, 22, London**

This sense of pride in themselves was often born out of having overcome some problem, to have 'put myself back together again'. Pride was to be found in doing those things that are widely understood to be leading a normal adult life. These included getting a job and paying rent on time. For others it was not taking drugs and keeping out of prison.

*What I think I am proud of is the fact that I have kept my head above the water. I mean I have been in a lot of difficult situations over the past couple of years but I didn't do the drug dealer or be on the streets just because I didn't have any money but there were times when it was really hard but also didn't go to violence towards myself or other people but I haven't really done much since. One thing I have never been on the street which is really good, you know, like I have been in bad hostels but not endangered myself by sleeping rough, you know. I think that's about it.* **May, English-Irish, 23, London**

Many of those who had children saw them as a strong source of identity and pride: 'the biggest part of my life ever'. Most, however, were not currently living with their children.

Self-identity also included personal interests or hobbies. In particular, those interested in sports such as football or snooker felt these were important aspects of their character. For those more creatively inclined, their writing or music was important to their identity.

## Identity and aspiration

When asked about goals and aspirations, the majority of young people interviewed one to one talked in terms of wanting a 'normal life'. For most this was to have a home, a family and a job. Others added nice holidays and a car. They pointed out that they were not looking for extravagant dreams: as one tellingly put it, they wanted to be 'integrated into society'.

*I've not got any plans, but hopefully I want to start off by getting a job. Right now I'm in a relationship and if that carried on I want to have a family, really to have a part-time job and be a housewife and a mother. I don't really want too much, normal things.*
**Sharon, Scottish, 24, London**

*I'd like to complete college, get a nice job, be integrated into society and just lead a normal life.* **David, White British, 24, London**

*I just want to do the same as everybody else. So like people say, "What do you want out of life?" If I had a choice of having anything, all I want is a house, me girlfriend – or*

*my wife to be – children and a nice job. And that's it. That's all I want out of life. Other people say they want millions and millions of pounds and I want this and I want that.*
**Tony, Devon**

Happiness was vitally important and very much a part of getting a normal life. In particular this depended on relationships.

*Why I want to be a mother and housewife? Because I love kids and I want to have a happy relationship, a relationship with a man because I've never had one, a happy one that is.* **Sharon, Scottish, 24, London**

*I don't know, it's really odd because I've always had this kind of, like, the perfect little world. It would be me and my husband and our children and our house and our car and our dog and our cat, do you understand, and that would be it and I would be happy. I would have a career but my family would come first which is kind of odd because my parents are separated and have been for like years and years and we went through loads of you know trauma and stuff, but I'm like really adamant that it can work, that I can have this perfect family, so that's it. I suppose, yeah, that's it…. I want to have good relationships with people. I want to have a better relationship with my children than my mother has with me, because although I admire her and I respect her a lot, we're not really close. That's it.* **Lynda, African, 20, London**

Some also aimed for particular jobs, such as becoming a cartoonist, social worker, musician or journalist. For some it was felt important to leave a 'legacy', to have achieved something in life. Some wanted to have helped others who had been in the same situation as themselves. As one explained, 'I've been through the pain of childhood and that and I don't want other children to go through that.' To achieve these ambitions some felt they needed support and, for work in particular, they felt they needed advice and guidance.

*I've got low self-esteem and I think, "Oh, I'm never gonna do this" and I give up. Unless I've got someone there egging me on saying, "Of course you can, of course you can", I'm gonna go for it. I won't do it for myself, I'll do it for someone else. If they say, "Oh go and do that for me", "Go to college, get your qualifications, for me", I'll do it, but I won't do it for myself. I've asked myself to do it and I can't.* **Beth, 17, London**

Despite these ambitions, for many the idea of the future and of planning for the future was difficult. Although they had clear ambitions, young people were keen to 'take one step at a time'. Planning for more than a few years at a time was considered difficult as 'anything might happen'. Equally, some felt afraid to plan in case things did not work out.

Understandably many were concerned with getting a home and 'stability' before they felt able to plan.

*I wouldn't say "plans". I'm hoping to get my own place and be working properly, then hopefully try to go through with a bit of education. Hopefully, I can do it along the way. There's a way to balance it out. At this present moment in time it would be for accommodation and so once that's settled then I can think more in the long run.* **Nick, London**

*What do I want to achieve in my life? Permanent accommodation, permanent job, permanent relationship, and maybe kids.* **John, White British, 25, London**

A few saw their past as an obstacle to achieving their goals and then it was something they would have to overcome. For example, one person who had a 'dream' of being a fireman was concerned that his drug history would prevent him from becoming one. Others were more positive.

*I mean you can spend your life wallowing in the past, can't you, and you could just get stuck in there. What's happening today, I mean you hear more about what's happening a couple of years ago, oh I wish I'd done this, oh what if this happens and all that, and in the end of it you just have a nervous breakdown. There won't be no future for you.* **Simon, Black British, 21, London**

Others believed that looking to the future was a way of overcoming the past.

*To have a bright future. What is happening to me now. I want it to be in history, to be a history for me.* **Susa, Nigerian, 19, London**

For many, thoughts of the future were very difficult. For them, the future was a 'black hole' and impossible to consider. One person commented that he might have children but would be dead before they grew up. Talking to those who felt this way was very difficult, with the young people giving one word negative replies and being unwilling or unable to think about possible aims.

*No there is no future. [How are you going to live next year then?] I'm going to get stoned out of my head. I'll OD.* **Mark, 20, London**

*I just think about how I'm going to get through this day. I don't think about next week or two weeks or whatever.* **Dana, Black, 18, London**

# Family, households and adulthood

## Findings

The issue of family and family relationships was raised again and again by young people during the course of this consultation. It was discussed in the context of belonging, identity, the transition to adulthood and in many other contexts. For most, it remained the primary source of their ideas about work, their attitudes to education and, for some, their political beliefs and class identities.

*First is my family – my mum, dad, sisters, brothers and my nan. My nan was the best friend I ever had since I was a kid. Without my family I have nothing.* **Rudy**

*My foster mum – without her I don't think I'd be the way I am now. I've been seeing her since I was five and she's taught me the right way to learn rather than being with my brother and my dad all the time.* **Kitty (both Oxford)**

When asked what gives you a sense of belonging, family and friends were again the focus.

*A home to go to, that you can lock the door behind you and feel safe and have your worries outside your door not inside. The stupid things that your mam keeps like your first shoes, your first drawing, your first school report. It makes you feel like you're wanted. Not that I am now like but it did then. Family surroundings like photographs, friends and people, you know.* **(Durham)**

Those who felt let down by family were deprived of this sense of belonging and several commented on the lack of boundaries that this had given them.

*Some of us would like to have been able to have been dependent on their parents, but it wasn't possible.* **(Edinburgh)**

*I did have [good parents] ... well I do, but they don't care what I do. I'd rather my mother and father said to me, "In by eleven o'clock" but they don't.*

*When I was locked up my mother wouldn't come and get me out, she said you stupid little bitch who wouldn't speak to me and then I thought no, it's like a cry for help, isn't it, I want you.* **(Cardiff)**

*I can see that a lot of my friends became socially excluded because of problems with their parents. I didn't leave my parents, they left me.* **(Edinburgh)**

### Family structure and conflict

Changes in family structure have a profound effect on young people, particularly with regard to one of the most important transitions to adulthood – leaving the family home. As one young person in the Edinburgh group commented, 'Everything seemed to come at once – trying to grow up and the family breaking down and getting hassle at school and all that.'

For many Real Deal participants, leaving home was less about a taking a willing step towards adulthood and more about family breakdown or strife. One young person in Edinburgh said the main advice she would give to another young person would be, 'Don't leave home unless you absolutely have to'. For some, independent living was often something they felt forced into before they were ready and also something that they had often not been supported to prepare for.

*I was at college and then I fell out with my mother over my step-dad. Then I moved into supported accommodation, where they had outpatients from Carstairs upstairs. I remember being able to hear the fighting during the day. They'd get their medication and then ten minutes later they'd be out the door trying to sell it. Could hear fighting, things getting broken and people being thrown about. One day I came back and there was a big pool of blood in the stairwell. No one would tell us what happened. They've closed those flats down now. But it seemed to me the situation was just under control and you felt that it could go at any minute. I was sixteen at the time.*

*My transition to independence probably started when I was about ten and was the first time I told my ma to "fuck off". She booted me out of the house and she wouldn't let me back in. I went to stay with pals for about a week and then from there into care, out of care, back into care. Jail, out of jail, in jail again. The first time I was really independent I was fifteen and I had a job and a car and I was staying in Glasgow East End. Could get any drugs you wanted without a prescription. (Edinburgh)*

Family breakdown and particularly relationships with step-parents were often a source of conflict.

*I started when I was fifteen. I moved out when I was sixteen. My mum took up with "the missing link" and the man will always be an arse. He'll be an arse till the day he dies. I knew I couldn't move out when I was fifteen and I didn't really know what to do. I got to sixteen. "Am I staying or not staying?" Things just started to get worse and then they got really bad. I wouldn't say I left entirely voluntary but there was really no way I could stay, so I moved out. (Edinburgh)*

*But my experience in my family was that my parents split up very acrimoniously. Oh it was horrible, a horrible experience. I was about fourteen at that time when they split up. I couldn't understand what the hell was going on because I only heard the shouting and the fighting and the whole weird situation around me. But I wasn't involved in it because I was told to get out and go away and that whole thing had such a drastic effect on my life as well because I couldn't understand what was going on, I wasn't being told what was going on. There was this pulling of sides and this questioning that I used to get, like, "What is your mother doing tonight?" (Aberdeenshire)*

Given the difficulties of this transition, the notion of independence sometimes rang hollow.

*Then some friends started to depend on me and that really freaked me out cos I wasn't able to look after myself never mind these other people. So I moved down to Aberdeen and in with my mother cos I just didn't know what else to do and then she moved out and I suppose that was the most independent time I've ever had. I had a flatmate who dealt drugs and she could get money and it was pretty easy to be out of my face most of the time. (Edinburgh)*

Others commented that their inability to depend on family and friends in some cases meant that they had to depend more on social services. For most this was problematic, partly because by the time they had reached that situation problems were mounting up.

> *X: There needs to be total family breakdown before they'll help you.*
> *Y: There doesn't seem to be any safe place to go and you always have to prove that you need help.*
> *X: You become dependent on the system.*
> *Y: You have to start getting good at finding the loopholes to keep any kind of independence. (Edinburgh)*

For others, independence simply meant isolation.

> *I don't think you are ever really independent. Everybody needs somebody. It's so hard when you're so young. I was sixteen. You can't get a decent wage. I'll always be dependent on somebody. I don't want to be totally independent. (Camberwell)*

Other young people felt that leaving home was not a necessary step towards adulthood. This is partly because some of the issues that had encouraged previous generations to want to leave, such as having some privacy, being able to have a sex life, staying out late and so on, had ceased to be contentious in their parental homes.

> *YC: Just before my eighteenth, around my eighteenth birthday as well, I'd got to the stage now where a boyfriend can just come home and it's accepted by Mum and Dad. I used to babysit because I was going steady. I didn't have to be in the house until 2.00 or 2.30am. Now I don't come home until ten the next morning – I just say, don't expect me in.*
> *Interviewer: Can I ask the other girls, I know you go out with fellas but would your parents mind if you stayed out all night?*
> *CC: I'm allowed to stay out all night.*
> *X: It's only now that I'm eighteen.*
> *KD: I will when I'm eighteen too.*
> *YC: It's a whole thing about trust as well because I was going steady and I wasn't staying out late. Whenever I was thirteen or fourteen, before I was going steady, I would have drunk a while lot and was never caught drinking. But then whenever I was going steady I never drunk that much and the fella I was going out with he was three years older than me and I was all trusted and all. They just began to trust me, I'd never done anything for them to say "we don't trust you". My older sister, whenever she was about seventeen or eighteen she got pregnant and my wee sister, she's just a bad'un like, so they trust me and that's just the way it is. Whether they should or not I don't know.*
> *Interviewer: What do they think you do when you stay out all night?*
> *YC: I just say I'm going to a party or something and that's fair enough. (Derry)*

## Leaving care

Many of the young people had experience of the care system. Managing money in particular was seen as a problem.

> *Rachel: I was seventeen when I left the care system and I got my own flat and stuff and I found it canny hard. You've got so many problems, you've got all your bills and you can't afford to pay them and you will think, no.*
> *Smithy: For me and Chunk, if we left the care system, we would be pretty much fucked cos like we wouldn't have a clue.*
> *Lisa: I wouldn't have a clue.*
> *Smithy: Everything is provided for us, all the money we need.*
> *Marzy: What I'd do is take an interest in what my parents do, what have they to do to like keep their lives running so that everything doesn't collapse.*
> *Smithy: So do you mean taking an interest in what they spend their money on, how they pay the bills and stuff like that?*
> *Marzy: If you just sort out a system in your head, like that money has to go to that.*
> *Smithy: But we can't do that in the care system. We get around £200 a week, and we don't have a clue what that gets spent on, they don't tell us how to budget money, we get around £7 a week for bus fares. (Durham)*

> *Some people when they leave home and the care system they just drop everything. I was at college and then as soon as I left I dropped everything. You're just wanting more money anyway so you're trying to get yourself a job but you're dropping college at the same time. The care system kept me going, the key worker and all the staff and that, but as soon as I left everything was dropped cos I didn't get no help. Rachel (Durham)*

Others also argued that the transition to leaving care was not well managed by the authorities and that in fact the care system had ceased to provide any sort of support for them long before they left.

> *The care system right, there's just no one really bothering about how you do at school, just as long as you don't cause trouble. They couldn't do anything to you anyway. They couldn't ground you or anything like that.*

> *When you're about fifteen in care the staff really don't bother you. They might when you are thirteen or fourteen, but by fifteen it doesn't matter so much.*

> *I think I've always had to be pretty independent cos I never had much of an upbringing. I was always being brought up by someone else's parents. Then the Social Work Department brought me up. Once they had finished with me I had to get two psychologists, a psychiatrist and a probation officer. The Social Work Department have a great policy – as soon as you turn sixteen that's you, you're buggered. After that they just dropped me, no support and they left me with a drug problem as well. They just left me there, in one of the worst areas of Glasgow, which was really nice of them. (Edinburgh)*

*I went on independent living at Peterlee, and all they done was say right there's £15 go and get your shopping in. £15 to get a week's shopping in. Considering I'm a cook right, I should know what to cook. Fair enough I could go and buy a chicken and this that and the other, but there's your £15 gone just by buying a chicken and some veg.* **Smithy (Durham)**

## Family, friends and children

The young people were asked about what they viewed as the ideal living for a young adult. Some found the idea of living alone unwelcome,

*I think sharing with a partner or friends is best, cos of the bills and the social support.* **Jen**

*Me and Chunk are thinking about living together when we leave the care system, because we can get more for the flat. Cos when you leave the care system, right, I know this sounds really shocking cos some parents can't afford it, but we get £1000 leaving care grant and you cannot get a lot for a £1000.* **Smithy**

*I didn't have my mates round all the time, I was always around my mates anyway. It was a waste of time me having a house I should have moved in with them. You get morbid in the house on your own.* **Rachel**

*There is a bit of a difference from the care system to moving into your own house because when you're in the care system you can guarantee there is anything happening at any time, you are never bored. But when you get your own place well you are like well what am I doing now, the phone isn't ringing, the police aren't around, nobody's running around, I'm not getting called for my tea, this, that and the other.* **Smithy (all Durham)**

While others welcomed it.

*I can't share with anyone else. I'd kill them. I shared with my brother for six months but I just can't get on sharing. If they don't do the dishes and stuff I go mental. My kitchen is always sparkling.*

*I didn't like sharing and got into problems over bills. Then they became a couple and it ended up two against one. I used to put their dirty dishes in their room for them to come home to.*

*I need my own space and I think everyone does.* **(Edinburgh)**

The young people also discussed the issue of relationships, marriage and children. For most, relationships and children was something they expected to have in their future. Very few felt that simply having sexual relationships was a sign of adulthood. Many noted that, with a high rate of teenage pregnancies, some people who are not adults are parents, but others argued that being a parent would help induce a sense of responsibility that was part of being an adult. As Emily from the Hull group put it, 'If you've got a kid you need to keep it together'.

> *Steve: I would say I've still got a way to go to be an adult, although I have had experiences which gave me an idea of what adult life is like. I was living with someone so I got to know what it was like, paying the bills and all. But I reckon maybe when I get married and have kids and a mortgage, then I'll be an adult.*
> *Interviewer: What if you don't get married?*
> *Steve: I will and have children.*
> *Interviewer: But suppose you don't meet anyone?*
> *Steve: Then I'll adopt, then I'll be an adult. (Derry)*

Some of the young people in the Oxford group were refugees, forced to live away from their families. While some spoke highly of their foster parents, they still viewed family as a strong source of support.

> *I think it has a very good impact on your life, having children. I reckon without children you haven't got no one. You've got to have children to support. You shouldn't forget that one day you might get old and you might need people to really care for you. Billy (Oxford)*

Some of the young people who were parents had more mixed views. Being a parent gave you a sense of responsibility, but could increase your dependence on others.

> *I thought I was really independent, but I realise now that I wasn't. I moved out when I was fifteen. The first time I was really independent was when I had my first baby. I'm still not that independent. I need to rely on my parents a lot.*

> *I wouldn't say I was that independent now. I have my own house and that but I'm dependent on people to babysit. That's my main issue. I need people to help me out with that. If I didn't have a child I could do my own thing. I don't have any regrets though. (Edinburgh)*

In contrast to what they see as the attitudes of settled people, the Traveller community still places huge important on family, particularly marriage. Officially, pre-marital sex is frowned upon and a young woman found to be sleeping with a boyfriend before marriage can be 'shunned' and lose the chance of marriage.

> *Traveller girls do not go out with boys. If a Traveller boy sees a girl at a wedding he likes, he will speak to her father. If the father agrees, the couple will go out together but they will not be left on their own until they get married. (Belfast)*

In the Traveller community, marriage and parenthood were clearly seen a signs of adulthood, indeed it was felt to be difficult to be considered an adult outside of that situation. One of the young women however, pointed out the distinction between being an 'adult' and being a 'woman'.

> *B: I think Traveller women become adults when they get married and have a big crowd of children. G —, now, she's not a woman but she's classed as an adult. She does every-thing that a woman does in the house, like look after children and cook and clean and all there, but she's not a woman.*
> *Interviewer: So when will she be a woman then?*
> *B: She'll be a woman when she gets married. She's getting married in eight months to my brother. She'll be a woman when she gets married and has a big crowd of small chil-dren under her feet. (Belfast)*

For young men in the Traveller community too, marriage is synonymous with attaining full adult-hood.

> *If the engagement goes well, you are expected to marry at seventeen and after that you are a man. You are expected to set up your own home and job and look after your wife and you will be helped by the parents to get independent, but by the time you are twenty your are on your own and it is hard to get help from anyone.*

> *Once you are engaged you will be welcome to be with the men and one of the greatest thrills is for a boy to be asked by the men to come to the pub and join in their talk. You feel on top of the world. At this stage the parents will let you in on the family secrets and give you information that would be important to your life in the family. Family history is explained and you are given warning about the behaviour of others and this is to be kept secret. If you go tell stories, you are cut out of the company. [If someone does not want to get married] that is difficult. If you have a reputation of being different then you are shunned. (Belfast)*

## Conclusions

These discussions threw up a wide range of themes, issues and views. They show that these young people are aware of the complex influences which shape their identities, and the ways in which their life experience conditions their view of community, family and adulthood. Despite the wide-rang-ing discussion, some clear conclusions can be drawn from what the Real Deal participants said.

■ The traditional idea of 'community' as a source of local belonging and involvement draws little sympathy or recognition. Many of these young people have had to move from the areas in which they grew up. Those more rooted in particular neighbourhoods often felt that they were not healthy communities, affected as they are by crime, poverty, drugs and unemployment.

■ The sense of community as a secure place where a sense of individual identity can be forged was often lacking. These young people felt a strong sense of exclusion and isolation from the wider 'community'. This sense was most clear and consistent among the homeless young people involved in one to one interviews.

■ Youth is an important source of identity, but many felt that it contributes to their sense of exclusion because of the discrimination and misperceptions of others.

■ Despite their rejection of traditional community, there was shared recognition of the importance of mutual support, care and commitment. The idea of community most strongly endorsed was grounded in the idea of belonging to a group of people with similar ideas, experiences and circumstances. Many had found a sense of community among those who are also excluded from the mainstream.

■ Communities are often associated with interference, and being recognised and respected as individuals is vitally important to many of these young people. Only the young people from the Traveller community felt any strong attachment to a traditional idea of community and family. Most felt that this way of life was under threat.

■ Outward signs and symbols are very important to a sense of belonging and identity. This includes dress, language and behaviour, and often contributes to young people's sense of isolation. Many of these young people feel pressured by youth media and consumer marketing, but do not have the means or money to participate in this way. National identity was not hugely important to most of the young people, although it was more so in Scotland. There was a widespread sense of national identity going through a period of change and of there being different levels of belonging and identification.

■ Family is fundamental to a sense of identity and belonging. Many said that family life was the most important influence on their perception of themselves. Many also felt that their negative experiences of family life made it more difficult to belong to a wider community, although most do not blame their parents or families for this.

■ Family plays a very important part in most people's hopes for the future. Awareness of responsibilities towards others shone out clearly from the discussions, although it was often tempered by a sense of alienation and abandonment.

■ Adulthood is a state of mind rather than a particular, age-related event. It is associated with responsibility and achievement, but not strongly with particular responsibilities. Adulthood was rarely seen defined by freedom, independence and choices.

■ For many, achieving adulthood was seen as difficult and complex. Many felt unsupported in preparing for life in the adult world. This was especially true for those who had lived in the care system or experienced homelessness.

■ Many felt that they were held back by past experiences and current circumstances. They were strongly determined to use their experience to make things better for themselves and others in the future.

■ These young people's aspirations for the future are no different from most other people's. They revolve around achieving positive relationships, stable homes, work and family. Many find it difficult to see how they will achieve these goals.

# What we do

## Leisure and Recreation

### Background

As a term, 'leisure' suggests many things. It can imply rest and relaxation, as well as competitive and creative pastimes. Leisure and recreational activities include both active and sedentary pastimes, either physical or cerebral, alone or with other people, in the home or outside it.

Leisure and recreational time is far more than just 'time off'. It functions as a vital means for personal fulfilment and development, both emotional and physical. With the growth of the leisure, tourism, fashion and arts industries, the benefits of active leisure are becoming ever more relevant to career prospects and social networks.

There are many ways, both direct and indirect, in which active use of leisure time can enhance young people's lives. In many cases it helps develop practical skills. More generally, it can provides contexts and opportunities for developing interpersonal awareness and abilities, and can provide beneficial exposure to networks of opportunity. Problem-solving and lateral thinking can be learned through constructive use of leisure time. Leisure activities can also extend a broader 'feel good factor'; they may promote better health, an improved environment and offer alternatives to anti-social behaviour.

Alcohol and drug use also play a regular part in many people's leisure lives. Recreational drugs are a universal presence among Britain's young people. Increasingly, they are available at lower prices, to people of a younger age. They are a mainstream element of youth culture. It was also found, in 1996, that record levels of eighteen to 24 year olds were exceeding their recommended weekly consumption of alcohol, with 41 per cent of men exceeding 21 units and 24 per cent of women exceeding fourteen units of alcohol.[12]

Understanding what Real Deal participants think about leisure, and what they do with their time, is an integral part of understanding their lives. How does lack of money impact on what people do? What do they enjoy most? Is there any distinction between leisure and other time if you are not working or in education?

# Findings

Many participants, particularly those who are unemployed, had a hard time separating leisure activities from the rest of life. Although some of the younger participants suggested lists of activities, the discussions revealed a strikingly narrow range of leisure activities, particularly organised ones, in which most people took part. Many said that they took part at all in organised sport. Lack of participation in organised leisure was allied with a view that local leisure facilities were 'crap' or overpriced. Some young people found it difficult to identify local facilities.

When asked what prevented them from taking part, distance, money, lack of public transport, responsibilities as parents or carers, disabilities and age restrictions were all mentioned. However, some young people said that lack of participation in organised leisure sprang more from inclination than from anything else.

Many young people said that they had a lot of time on their hands. In some cases this was occupied by drinking, illegal drugs and, for a minority, crime, particularly car crime. Given the low incomes of many Real Deal participants, drinking and drug taking were occasional activities, limited partly by the amount of money they had to spend, and a lot of time was spent just hanging about.

Many participants expressed appreciation of the facilities offered by the youth clubs or centres in which the Real Deal discussions took place. More particularly, they were grateful to have people to talk to at the centres rather than leisure facilities as such.

## What is leisure?

For those in school or work, defining leisure as what you did with the rest of your time was somewhat easier than for those who are unemployed.

> *It's what you do in your spare time, it's what you do in your free time away from school.*
> *(Cardiff)*

> *D: Leisure is activities as well, isn't it?*
> *Interviewer: That can't be true that all your life is spent doing leisure.*
> *Penfold: But it's not working, is it, really?*
> *Interviewer: But would you consider your lifestyles 100 per cent leisure – is none of it stressful, things you don't want to do?*
> *Stu: Leisure is what you want to do, ain't it? And all we do all day is what we want to do.*
> *Penfold: Listen, leisure is doing the things you like, and we do what we like every day, so that must be our leisure. (Hull)*

Most groups came up with a long list of possible leisure activities including bowling, cinema, pubs, clubs, watching TV, drinking, phoning friends, shopping, computers, ice skating, football, bikes, computer games, visiting friends, listening to or playing music and fishing. In more detailed discussion however, it appeared that some, particularly those who had left school and were unemployed, actually took part in relatively few of these activities. Only television, drinking and visiting friends were things that most of the young people took part in. Individuals mentioned activities, but there was little consensus and many of the activities below were mentioned by a minority.

A few, particularly those who had lived abroad, mentioned travelling as a leisure activity that they aspired to.

> *I would love to go to places like visit places I've never seen before in Oxford and London. I've been to some places but I'd like to have time to go to more places especially in London and any other parts of England.* **Ab (Oxford)**

> *I would spend a lot of time outside of Derry. I would go to Belfast maybe once every two weeks. I go to Claudy and I go to Dublin and Portrush. I find I don't go out much in Belfast.* **YC (Derry)**

For a few of the young people, crime was a major leisure activity and it was seen as leisure, not just because it happened in 'spare' time, but because it gave them a buzz or feeling of enjoyment.

> *T: TWOCing [taking without consent] it's driving isn't it ... it's a hobby, isn't it, for some people.*
> *P: It's more like an addiction.*
> *T: No, it's a hobby for some people ... go up and you'll see them driving around in brand new Mercs and everything what they've just nicked. And they don't pinch 'em like we pinch 'em.*
> *Q: Stealing cars, it isn't a sport.*
> *T: It's like a hobby then, it's an addiction to earn money.*
> *D: You get two kinds of car thieves don't you. You get car thieves that do it for money and car thieves who do it for fun.*
> *P: Both do it because they are addicted to it.*
> *T: I'm not addicted to it, but I still do it.* **(Hull)**

One young woman, who did not wish to be involved in taking cars, enjoyed going to be a spectator.

A common theme emerging from the group discussions was that many of the young people felt they needed 'a challenge' as a way to stimulate and motivate them. As one young man put it, 'sports are good if they are competitive'. Several reported having played for school teams. Others in the Edinburgh group discussed the buzz of 'performing'.

> *X: Another good one, although not quite as good as sex, but quite good instead of drugs, is drama. When I was doing choir, going up on stage is an amazing feeling when you've got 200 folk appreciating what you've done. You're standing on a stage and when you*

*finish a show, you feel absolutely amazing.*

*Y: Yeah, it is a major, major buzz. I used to get a huge buzz if I played and the crowd would be shouting your name at the end of the night. I used to end up hiding behind the decks, with my face going bright red, rushing off my head on adrenaline, going "please tell them to shut up".*

*X: It's a lift. It's a drug again. It makes you feel high, it makes you feel happy.*

*Z: I used to sing at school in musicals and I used to love it. At the end, if I'd done well and people used to clap, I just felt that someone was valuing what I'd done.*

Attitudes to the IT and computer games varied widely. Some young people enjoyed playing games and using the Internet, while others (perhaps the majority) were uninterested.

*The Internet's great, especially for young'uns, you can get into anything.* **Big Dunc, Durham group**

Some people felt more ambivalent about it.

*G: To get on to the Internet is going to cost you lots.*

*R: Not necessarily because you can reroute it. If you can get through on the Internet you can get news from all round the world, different news and you are not going to have it controlled by anyone – big brother.*

*G: They shouldn't have invented it. They invent all this stuff but they don't think of all the long-term effects of what is going to happen. On the Internet you can get child porn or whatever, you can learn how to make bombs. It is nuts.* **(Aberdeenshire)**

*Hoysey: There's more to do now.*

*Jen: Like what?*

*Hoysey: More Playstation …*

*Dunny: Consoles and more computers about. You've got like PCs and you can get in touch with the world on computer, can't you?*

*Bart: But it's a rip-off, you don't talk to people in America and that.*

*Q: Yes, you do.*

*Interviewer: Do you think people spend more time watching TV now and playing computer games and stuff like that?*

*Dunny: Nowadays people are getting lazy … computers are coming out … so they only bother with exercising their fingers aren't they.*

*Hoysey: What's going on, it's coming to the point where you don't even have to go outside to shop … there's all these shopping channels. You don't even have to go out to post a letter, if you've got a fax machine you just fax it … it's about changes.*

*Dunny: It's changes … it's all like digital and stuff like that. People are getting more lazy.* **(Hull)**

### Drugs

For most of the Real Deal participants, drinking and illegal drugs play a large part in their leisure time.

> *Drugs are quite a main factor in my leisure time, smoking dope or taking E, or taking speed or whatever. Personally, I don't do acid or anything else. But for most of my friends, most of the time when we are hanging out or having leisure time together, it is with drugs ... whether it's nicotine, alcohol or whatever. Drugs always seem to be there.* **(Edinburgh)**

Asked to describe an average day, one young person responded:

> *K: Dealers, chemist, hospital.*
> *Interviewer: What do you go to hospital for?*
> *K: To do it.*
> *Interviewer: To do what?*
> *K: The speed.*
> *Interviewer: At what hospital?*
> *K: Yeah, I do it in the toilets. They've got a needle place and I always clear up afterwards.* **(Hull)**

For a few, drug use replaces or interferes with other leisure activities.

> *Interviewer: What about sport – some of you lot have played sport. I know you have Chris and you P, you had a chance to turn pro football, didn't you?*
> *Penfold: Yeah, for Hull City.*
> *P: I had trials twice man.*
> *Interviewer: Do you think that if young people like yourselves get a chance to do well in sport, do you think it helps them?*
> *P: It does and it doesn't.*
> *Interviewer: What stopped you going all the way in football?*
> *P: Drugs.*
> *Penfold: He went to football trials smacked-up.* **(Hull)**

> *I actually think I wouldn't smoke so much dope if I had something else to do. It's not that I don't like it, cos I do like a smoke. But I don't just smoke because I need to smoke, I smoke cos I have nothing else to do and hating the job is part of that.* **TB (Derry)**

Those who are regular drug users are dismissive of government attempts to deal with the issue.

> *E: I think the government are going to have to accept that drugs are part of youth culture.*
> *X: It's here to stay.*

*Y: It is.*

*X: There's nothing they can do about it. It's never moved. It happened in the 60s.*

*Y: They've got to face defeat.*

*G: It's not really defeat. Well, it's defeat. Instead of coming down with all this heavy-handed stuff they should try and understand why young people take drugs which I suppose is why they are starting this project up and understand what young people are thinking and what they are doing with their spare time. Because it is, spare time that, standing around on street corners, doing nothing and you go and smoke a joint or you go and break into a house. That's why a lot of crime starts. Because young people have far too much spare time and they want something to give them a buzz to make it exciting.*
**(Aberdeenshire)**

There was not a strong consensus on this issue. It is noticeable that younger Real Deal participants were more likely to have a firm anti-drugs attitude. This was particularly apparent in the Oxford group, whose members were slightly younger and included some refugees from Africa. They tended to disapprove of drugs and in some cases, alcohol. For some, peer pressure to drink or use drugs can be a problem.

*Ab: I went to my friend's party – fourteenth birthday, I couldn't believe what was going on there – everyone was drunk, and they had to carry everyone about – I would never go to a party like this. They bought so many drinks they did it purposely to get drunk. They try to get on with someone they really fancy and they get drunk and make the person get drunk so that they can get off with them. I get so fed up it was a garden party – there was no music. I just went off dancing on my own they were all drunk – they were all drunk.*

*Tigger: Peer pressure isn't just people coming up to you and saying you will smoke, it's that everyone around you is doing it. If everyone around you is having a drink and you're not.*

*Deej: It's like with smoke, people keep passing it round – I just pass it on saying I've had enough even though I haven't had any.*

*Ab: They offer it to me – they know me but they want to watch us drinking.* **(Oxford)**

Others had become disillusioned or regarded drugs as a passing phase they would grow out of.

*Interviewer: You said you got depressed. Why?*

*E: I couldn't see where I was going in life. I suppose I just felt I couldn't spend the rest of my life drinking. I wanted to have a house and have all those things and that's what I opted for. It's like everything else. If you do the same thing every day for months on end you get sick of it, you would it doesn't matter what you do. The drugs and drinking stop having an effect and was boring. I was taking a lot of Es and I was taking the same as other people and I got nothing out of it. Eventually you're immune from it.*
**(Aberdeenshire)**

*D: I don't want to be a fucking druggie, a low life all the time.*
*P: But if we didn't like it we wouldn't do it.*
*Interviewer: So how do you think you might change that, D?*
*D: We're only young now.*
*Interviewer: So you think you'll change? In a few years ... or ...?*
*D: I'll grow out of it. (Hull)*

While others felt they drank as much as they did because there were few other leisure activities to replace it.

*It's hard to identify an alternative to the pub scene. I'm in the early stages. There's things I have identified I would like to do but I haven't got round to them yet. Like I've always been putting off writing – for most of my life I've felt I've got quite a good story in me, I just haven't got round to it yet. Other things like I could go and play pool on a Friday or Saturday night but everyone else is out drinking and there's not all that many people that I could play a decent match with, you know.* **Miles (Derry)**

For a minority, drug taking had been part of family life and reactions to this varied. One young person who had been introduced to drugs by their parents had firm views about not taking drugs in front of children,

*One thing that used to freak me out when I was younger was being at home, there was this lass upstairs with a bairn and she was out of her face the whole time with the bairn. Her daughter just used to wander down and be with me. I wouldn't let anyone take anything in front of her. Okay, they'd smoke a joint, but they weren't allowed to skin up in front of her. I know that sounds really strange but it doesn't seem so in your face, if someone isn't skinning in front of you or snorting in front of you. I don't see how you could do that to a bairn. I knew a three year old that could skin up for his parents.* **(Edinburgh)**

Others, however, had been introduced to drug taking by their parents. For some this was an encouragement while others felt they had 'seen the effects', and it had put them off.

*I found out that my mum and step-dad smoked hash when I was about eleven. Because I came home from school, having just been at the receiving end of a "just say no" campaign and I was like, "This drugs thing ... there are so many people dying, it's so bad." My mum just sat me down and said, "Right, let's have a discussion about facts and reality" and I discovered they had been smoking pot my entire life, since before I was born. They hadn't gone mad, they hadn't axed anyone to death, they weren't injecting anything. They were fairly normal people. It shook my whole view of the issue, but my only view of the issue was "Just say no, anti-everything, everything is evil". (Edinburgh)*

Drug use undoubtedly varied widely among the different Real Deal groups, as did attitudes to government policy on the issue. Among the older participants, drug use was widespread and, for a few, it had become a problem, leading to health risks, social problems and, in some cases, criminal offending. Others managed their drug consumption relatively successfully, while a significant minority of participants, particularly in the younger age groups, were firmly opposed to drug use and felt that government policy should reflect this.

## Socialising and friendship

Friends were the most important people to spend time with for most Real Deal participants. Meeting people and socialising with friends was regarded as one of the main benefits of leisure time. Not having friends or people to talk to was seen as one of the main reasons for boredom, as one of the refugees from the Oxford group explained:

> *In my old home where I used to live in my country I will say that I was living in a ghetto and I had lots of people to talk to; I'm comparing it with that. I had so much friends and were so popular I've never been bored in my life except when I came here. I just miss so much that. I've got no one to talk to. I've got friends in Oxford – they can't even be bothered to come all the way to Abingdon, a boring place to talk to me, so I end up getting a bus always. I don't have a choice, or I have to sit down at home bored or come down here. I miss it … I know if I had more friends I wouldn't sit watching TV all day.*
> *Ab*

> *A: At the end of the day, we're bored. We haven't got a home to go to, no family, that's why.*
> *Emily: If we was being occupied all the time, activities to do …*
> *A: That's why I treat my mates as a family.*
> *Stu: It's right, that's why I do.*
> *A: My mates come first and that's right – that's why I've never got money.* *(Hull)*

For the Traveller groups, leisure time was often spent with family members. However, very few people in other groups mentioned their families as people they liked to spend their leisure time with. Conflict with families about how to spend leisure time was discussed,

> *Interviewer: How much influence do you parents have on how you spend your free time or your leisure time?*
> *X: Personally they don't care, as long as you're not in the fuckin' house.* *(Belfast)*

The belief that crime had increased since their parents' day and hence that they were more constrained in where they could go was expressed by some of the younger people.

> *My mother won't let me go camping, don't trust me, well not just me though I think a lot of things with camping is that people [like] Sophie Hook got murdered.* *(Cardiff)*

Many of the young people spoke highly of the youth clubs and facilities where these discussions were taking place and more particularly of the people who were there for them to talk to.

*RAPP's the only place that pays for us to go anywhere. There's no one else that's bothered about us. No one else takes us anywhere, only RAPP. People think we're daft. **Emily** (Hull)*

*Interviewer: To get back to this question, what else would you improve in Hull, if you could go to the City Council and say "this is what we want to see happen" what would you say?*
*Penfold: A better Warren – more places like the Warren.*
*Emily: More places [like] the Warren and RAPP.*
*Chris: A 24/7 Warren.*
*Interviewer: What's that?*
*Chris: Twenty-four hours a day, seven days a week. **(Hull)***

*X: And everyone comes here because they know they can relax and like everyone will make you welcome – do what you want.*
*Y: No stress from parents.*
*X: And plus everything that goes on in this youth centre is confidential. **(Cardiff)***

This positive experience had led to many of the young people working voluntarily in the centres, either as peer educators or other helpers. Many others suggested that more such places should be made available for young people and that they should be open later and longer.

Perceived gender differences in leisure activities seemed to be fading. Most who were asked felt that there was little difference between how men and women spend their leisure time. A few argued that men were more likely to do sport.

*Ab: I think so, boys they have football to deal with ... [laughter]*
*X: They can just go and find some people playing football and say, "Can I join you?" and they are allowed to. But with girls you think, gosh, are they going to tell me to get off? **(Oxford)***

### Organised leisure facilities

The young people were asked how they felt about organised leisure facilities in their areas and how aware they were of what was on offer. Most were unimpressed by local leisure facilities: either they felt there was not enough to do or, more often, they felt organised leisure facilities were too expensive. Age restrictions and the feeling that they were not welcome at certain venues added to these feelings, and in some cases became a barrier to use.

*They are too expensive, too far to travel to and that costs money too! **Lisa***

*There are not enough options. **Tanya***

*Age has a lot to do with it too. A lot of stuff is not aimed at our age group, it's either for children or people like me mum!* **Zoe (all Durham)**

Others felt they were looked down upon in some more expensive venues.

*I think they're hostile to young people, depending on where you come from. If you walk in and they think you're not intending to go on anything (you just want to go in and spectate, which you can do), they say get to the canteen and don't come out because you're not spending any money. I think they are quite hostile to young people. At least the one where I used to live in … was terrible. The staff were really mean. If you were going in swimming they were fine, but if you just wanted to spectate they just told you to get to the canteen.* **(Edinburgh)**

Other young people pointed out that the fifteen to seventeen age group was particularly ill-served by organised leisure facilities, too old for youth clubs, too young for pubs and clubs. As one young man in Derry pointed out:

*I know it's hard, but most people have nothing to do when they're too old for youth clubs, and that's at thirteen or fourteen, then it's just the pub. There's nothing else to do. There's a big gap.*

Real Deal participants felt that organised leisure facilities concentrate too much on sport, to the exclusion of other things.

*If you don't like sports or anything like that then you aren't going to use the courts you haven't got any other facilities to go to – you need to get out of St Mellons to go to other facilities. And most people don't like staying in St Mellons all the time because it just gets boring and you're doing the same thing all the time.*

*You end up getting into trouble then if you just carry on roaming the streets and that.* **(Cardiff)**

*X: They cater for those who enjoy sports, I suppose. That's about it. Or dancing.*
*A: There does seem to be an over-abundance of leisure facilities in Alba if you are into sport.*
*Y: And you've got the money to pay for it.*
*X: Yeah, aye.*
*Y: If you're unemployed, you're nae going to spend the money you've got on pumping a few weights. Sod that, stupid.* **(Aberdeenshire)**

Other people were dismayed by the lack of 24-hour leisure facilities, even in big cities.

*X: We used to traipse around graveyards at midnight, because there was nothing else to do we were so bored. It was better than being in the house.*

*Y: We had Café Insomnia in Glasgow [a 24-hour café].*

*Z: It's the only 24-hour place and it's £1.20 for a cup of tea. And you have to queue. It's all right because it is something to do but you do need the money. You're sitting there and you feel excluded because everyone is sitting there, they have all been out and they're all steaming and they are all fighting about who's paying the bill and taking out £50 notes from their purse.* **(Edinburgh)**

The two London groups were asked to design their own leisure centre. Suggestions varied, but several of the young people wanted a resource centre, 'a leisure centre with learning facilities', rather than just a recreation centre. A key concern was to create a venue which filled a gap rather than facilities that were considered widely available such as discos and cinemas.

*We don't want a cinema. There are plenty of cinemas and they are too expensive anyway.* **(Buffy House)**

Existing local existing facilities were not used or perceived to be inadequate for a number of reasons: people who used the facilities were not young, the facilities were shabby or poor or the venue was seen as obscure or uninviting.

Ladbroke Grove in London was praised as an area having the 'right idea' about facilities for young people,

*They have lots of centres – burger bars, astro-turfs, different things.* **(Buffy House)**

Other groups were asked what recommendations they would give to policy-makers about recreational facilities. It is striking that many were keenly aware of the differences between themselves and more affluent groups.

*Interviewer: What would you like to see more of, or less of?*

*Emily: Lower prices.*

*Penfold: Fun fairs – free fun fairs.*

*Emily: More motorbike centres like Chapman Street.*

*Stu: Go-karting centres.*

*Interviewer: So there's not much for kids to do – is that what you're saying?*

*Emily: Yeah.*

*D: Some parents haven't got much money though.*

*Stu: It's all right for the posh little kids.*

*Interviewer: So, the posh kids, their parents can pay, but others can't – is that what you mean?*

*Emily/D/Stu: Yeah.*

*Craig: What's posh kids leisure activities in your view?*

*D: Go-karting.*

*Stu: Playing backgammon and that shit.*

*D: Going out for a big suit and playing chess.*

*Stu: It's all the cheap plastic stuff what we get, they get the real stuff, do you know what I mean? (Hull)*

Others felt that policy-makers should address age restrictions: that current rules were inconsistent and should be rationalised.

*They should try to change the structure of the way young people grow up cos you get to a certain age, you start going to the pub, or you start drinking anyway. Then you start into the draw. You know, you can see everyone has done more or less the same thing with their lives, social wise. I think they should try to get a better – I know it's hard but most people have nothing to do when they're too old for youth clubs, and that's at thirteen or fourteen, then it's just the pub. There's nothing else to do. There's a big gap.* **JQ (Derry)**

There was much scepticism that they would get what they wanted from politicians who were seen to prefer 'high profile' leisure spending.

*X: Yeah, but there is no point in going down that road again, because we have said that about 15 million times that we want a swimming pool and we never get it so there is no point.*
*Y: The politicians are focusing too much on the city centre and Cardiff Bay development and they aren't focusing much on the outskirts, ie St Mellons.*
*Z: Can you imagine someone comes over from abroad, goes to stay in the city centre and by accident they catches the no.62 to St Mellons they come down here and it's a completely different life, isn't it?*
*Y: But tourists as well it gives them a misleading sort of picture of Cardiff.*
*Z: Because they are only showing them the good side. (Cardiff)*

## Barriers to leisure and recreation

A range of barriers were cited to leisure and recreational activities. Chief among them was money, but distance and lack of public transport also played a part, especially for young people in rural communities.

*Hoysey: Travel – I'd say it's about where the actual places where you are going.*
*Skezz: Can't be bothered to wait for a bus to go to the area where you want to be.*
*Hoysey: They [the bus services] aren't good on Sundays. On Sundays definitely. The buses on Sundays should be every half an hour, not every hour. That's when I've got to get to matches and stuff.*
*Skezz: The bus services should be like they are on a weekday.*
*Hoysey: Cos that's when most of football is on ... Sunday league ... I've got to get to matches on Sundays and I've got to set off an hour before I should do. (Hull)*

*The trouble with sports facilities is that they are expensive – for a one-off yes, but if you want to go for regular exercise it's too expensive.* **Tigger (Oxford)**

Age often acts as a barrier for the young people and they felt squeezed from both sides – to young to take part in some leisure activities and too old to get cheap fares on public transport.

> *Cos as of sixteen you have to pay full fare and many of my friends have birthdays at the beginning of the year and still are in full-time education and that's something that really annoys me. For me its about £2 just to get into Oxford, so if I was going to have to pay that as well as paying to do anything within Oxford I would have no money at all.* **(Oxford)**

> **Ab:** *I would love to go to clubs – mainly for the dancing – it gives me a mind of being … when I dance or when I listen to music I forget about everything.*
> **Tigger:** *Clubs are really expensive.*
> **Ab:** *Is it sixteen you can go to club or eighteen?*
> **Tigger:** *Eighteen or some are 21.* **(Oxford)**

For some young people, even where leisure facilities were available, they did not feel part of them.

> **X:** *The Arcade, it's just empty.*
> **Interviewer:** *You used to have the pool hall?*
> **X:** *That was a long time ago.*
> **Y:** *It wasn't very big.*
> **X:** *But a lot of people fitted into it.*
> **Z:** *It was only certain people went into it.*
> **X:** *People like us.*
> **Z:** *Basically it was our pool hall.* **(Aberdeenshire)**

For some, being a parent or a young carer was a restriction on social life. This was particularly true for the young Travellers for whom family responsibility is a big obstacle to leisure time. They also often felt discriminated against in organised leisure facilities, not just by staff but by other young people.

When asked to design a leisure facility, the Camberwell group disagreed over what childcare provisions were required,

> *Being in this area no one has much money. There is a need for facilities for all, so you need childminding facilities because people need them. They need somewhere they can put their children, which is safe, cheap and local.*

> *We don't want childminding. If you want to come you should bring your kid with you. It's like leaving a dog, leaving your kid. You should take it with you … we don't want children crying.*

# Conclusions

■ The young people involved in the Real Deal did not participate in a wide range of structured leisure activities. Many found it difficult to differentiate between leisure time and other things.

■ Drugs and alcohol played a regular part in most people's routines. There was a clear distinction between older people, who felt that government messages about drugs were inappropriate and unrealistic, and younger ones who were more likely to adopt a 'just say no' approach.

■ Many feel excluded from mainstream leisure opportunities, primarily by money, but also by other people's attitudes and by inappropriate provision. Sport is not an attractive option for more than a small proportion.

■ The need for a 'challenge' or 'buzz' was clearly identified. Sources of excitement varied from performing to drugs to car crime. Many young people felt that existing recreational facilities did not offer this kind of stimulation.

■ Use of information technology was patchy, and discussion of the Internet was largely hypothetical. Equipment and access were difficult for many to find, largely because of cost.

■ Many mentioned boredom as one of the factors governing their use of time.

■ Accessibility and timing were key to creating alternative activities. Many young people felt that there was a gap between facilities for younger children and adult provision, and that safe, interesting places for teenagers were in short supply. Twenty-four hour facilities were strongly endorsed.

■ Having people to talk to and being treated with respect were at least as important as having physical spaces and facilities to use.

■ Transport and childcare were also significant barriers to leisure facilities.

# Learning and working

## Learning

### Background

Education has become one of the highest priorities for governments across the world over the last fifteen years. The radical changes we have seen are as much the result of changing social and economic conditions as of near-continuous reform. Alongside a focus on improving attainment within the school system, a new infrastructure for lifelong learning is being built, on the assumption that people will need to re-skill and change career far more often during their adult lives.

These wider changes have also had a dramatic impact on the world of work. Many jobs previously available to people without high levels of educational qualification have disappeared, in particular, jobs in manufacturing, construction and heavy industries. Although manufacturing is still very important to the British economy, the number of available jobs has shrunk.

The growth of new industries, particularly in service-based and knowledge-intensive sectors, means that educational qualifications are far more important to gaining employment than in the past. In addition, employers are increasingly looking for personal skills such as initiative, creativity, problem-solving and the ability to work collaboratively. In this sense, learning and work are being fused together, no longer pursued in separate institutions, but fitting into semi-continuous patterns of personal development. At the same time, a new focus on personal and interpersonal learning has appeared, as we recognise that emotions, relationships and active community membership are all things that we can learn to manage more effectively and are crucial to personal achievement and productive participation in society.

As a result, there has been steady progress towards greater participation in education. More young people get GCSEs and A levels, more participate in higher and further education, more are getting specialist technical qualifications. Over 70 per cent of young people in the UK now stay in learning beyond the age of sixteen and a third take part in higher education.

Despite this, while the leading edge of educational attainment in the UK accelerates, there are still serious problems of underachievement. As many as 15 per cent of 21 years olds have limited literacy skills and 20 per cent have difficulties even with basic maths. The proportion of young people leaving education at sixteen with no qualifications has remained a steady 7 to 8 per cent. In a world of increased competition and growing emphasis on knowledge-intensive work, young people who have not achieved in education are more likely than ever to be severely disadvantaged.

Education is fundamental to tackling social exclusion and emerged as a consistent theme throughout many of the Real Deal discussions. Government policy encourages work to be viewed in the same way, as essential not only to earning a living, but also to a fulfilling and productive life. Alongside the perennial desire to reduce expenditure on benefits, policies to reduce unemployment are justified on grounds of individual self-esteem and social cohesion. Work is central to the way many people see themselves: their ability to earn an income, their contact with others, their sense of self-esteem and their standing in the wider community.

But for societies to learn, and for individuals to become successful lifelong learners, experience and attitude are as important as the quality of courses and infrastructure. Many people who urgently need to develop their skills and knowledge have highly negative experiences of the education system, and this inevitably influences their attitudes to further learning. This often contributes to continued labour market disadvantage, since qualifications and training are often a prerequisite to stable employment.

Given their connection and importance, we have brought the themes of education and work together. The initial discussions centre on the young people's actual experience of school or formal education. Attitudes to education and work and their value are then discussed, as are influences on the young people's choices. We also look at specific policy ideas, including how the Real Deal participants felt that schooling could be improved and their reactions to recent government initiatives such as New Deal and the minimum wage.

## Findings

### *Experience of education*

Many of the young people found discussing education difficult, and reported bad experiences of school. Among those who agreed that education did have some benefits, many had a fairly utilitarian view of them. 'It equips you to get a decent job' was singled out as the major advantage.

> *If you haven't got an education you can't get a decent job. If you haven't got a decent job you can't earn decent money. And if you haven't got decent money then you won't have a decent anything, a decent house, a decent car.* **Chunk (Durham)**

> *You want to finish school and sit in an office and get paid £8 or £10 an hour or even more than that with just a pen and paper. It's what I want. I don't want to end up in a hard job and if you get no schooling you can't get what you want.* **Rudy (Oxford)**

Some did have other ideas.

> *You might not learn just for a job, you might want to learn for yourself.* **Lisa**

*Education is part of your community and your culture.* **Zoe**

*I think it helps you to develop a stronger mind.* **Christine (all Durham)**

Apart from the enjoyment of seeing friends, many young people recognised that going to school 'socialised' you at some level.

*I think young people need to go to school because, apart from going to school to get the education you get, people from different areas [are] in school and like, even if you wouldn't want to know them better, you are forced to because you are with them and you can't just ignore the fact that you are with them. You learn a lot from other people and you get to respect other people in a way you wouldn't do on the street.* **Deej (Oxford)**

*Social skills. I suppose if you were just around the streets, you wouldn't get to know people. If you are in school, you get to meet lots of people.* **Keith (Camberwell)**

School was the major experience most young people had had of formal education, so there was little discussion of informal or non-school education. This may also account for the fact that the idea of 'lifelong learning' was difficult to grasp for some. Those who had experience of post-school education such as college tended to view it more favourably than school, praising the greater informality, flexibility and, in some cases, responsibility that it entails.

Truancy and school exclusions were fairly common experiences among the groups, with several not really making the transition from primary to secondary school and attending only partially thereafter. Young people who had had problems at home or had been in care were likely to be in this group. Many expressed the view that the education system did not recognise how trauma and instability in their personal lives made them unable to focus on their education. As one young person in the Aberdeenshire group put it, 'Why did the teachers not pay more attention to the life situation I had to live through?' Many felt there was insufficient support for them within school.

Some young people were quite fatalistic about the chance for change in the education system and gloomy about the prospects for improving schools. Many complained they had not had a decent education, but found it difficult to articulate the reasons. As Emily from the Hull group explained, she wanted 'a good education like education is supposed to be. But I don't know what education is about or what it's supposed to be.' This degree of fatalism was not uncommon, but by no means universal. Others were full of suggestions for improving schools, including better training of teachers, wider curricula with an emphasis on life skills, more flexible time-tabling and improved counselling and support services.

For some young people the experience of school was almost totally negative.

*I had a crap time at school. I was called "stupid" and I used to ask teachers questions all the time and they didn't like me. When I came back to Scotland from England I was put into the wrong year. I went to loads of schools cos we moved house all the time.*

*Eventually [they] discovered that I was dyslexic. In primary schools I was sent to special ed teachers and they'd come up and take the pen off you. I'd say "but I can do that myself" and they wouldn't listen and I used to get really angry. I learnt a lot more when I left school. I went to Sixth Form College.*

*School? Totally crap. I learnt nothing of much use there. It just taught you to have no respect for teachers or the system. Everyone got signed in every 40 minutes to every class.* **(Edinburgh)**

For the Traveller community, accessing even basic education services can be difficult. Some go to school with 'settled' people, others to segregated Traveller schools. Some expressed the view that, despite the discrimination they often suffered, school with settled children could lead to higher attainment.

*It's better and then you could get mixed in with the settled people and know what kind of things they do and they'd put you through exams, the 11 Plus and all that.* **J (Belfast)**

One young person was asked if Travellers got as good an education as settled people.

*No, they don't get nothing like settled people. There is no right school for them. There is only the Travellers' Reader. "This is a car", "this is a lorry". They don't learn the same as settled people or put you through exams or nothing like that.* **B (Belfast)**

Some enjoyed school initially, only to be put off as they got older. The reasons for this varied from problems with learning to bullying, unsympathetic teachers and distractions such as drugs.

*I did fine in school because I was pretty bright and I only ran into problems when I started to question things. Then I just began to lose interest.* **(Edinburgh)**

*I think you go to school at the wrong time. It's set for the wrong age. When you are at school, I don't know about anybody else, but I never wanted to be there. But now I would quite happily go to school.* **John (Durham)**

In some cases, peer pressure not to be seen as a 'swot' was strong.

*There is no way I could have worked in any of my classes. I had a reputation to keep up and I couldn't show in any of my classes that I was smart. I had an agreement with the teachers. I'd never hand work in, but I'd do it later and give it to them separately and then ask them for the marks. I was basically about getting drunk and taking drugs and being a waster.* **(Edinburgh)**

When asked what were the best things about school, most said being with their friends and a few mentioned specific subjects they had enjoyed. For others, it was simply being a child and not having any adult responsibilities.

> **Interviewer:** *What was good about school?*
> **Lisa:** *Having a laugh with your friends ... PE.*
> **Chunk:** *IT.*
> **Christine:** *You are reckless, irresponsible and you haven't got any of the adult worries. You are still a child!*
> **Zoe:** *When you leave school at sixteen you are expected to become an adult overnight.*
> **(Durham)**

One young man from the Hull group summarised the reasons for not going to school as 'sex, drugs and hardcore'.

> *Well, sex you get pregnant yeah so you can't go to school. Drugs you just think "fuck it man, I'm out of me head, I'm not going to school" and when there's a rave on you say "fuck it, I'm off to this rave!" Simple.* **B**

Discussion of the worst things in school, or the problems encountered there, brought up a long list of issues. These included: teachers and their attitudes, bullying, drugs, violence, truancy and exclusion and learning difficulties.

## Teachers

For most young people in the groups, teachers were identified as a problem and one of the main barriers to improving education, although this view was not universal. Many felt that teachers were either not interested in them specifically because they were troublesome or uninterested in teaching in general.

> *In fact in some classes you had no pressure on you at all to do anything cos the teachers even knew you weren't interested and used to say, "Look just come to the class and get signed in so that I can make sure you're all right" and that's it.* **(Edinburgh)**

> *There were people in my class more brainy than me but they seemed to get more attention. If you stuck up your hand and said you were stuck, they said I'll come back later and they saw the other ones. That's why you got pissed off in classes.* **G (Aberdeenshire)**

Other complained that teachers made them feel stupid or humiliated them.

> *X: They just go about it the wrong way, because they try to embarrass you in front of the whole class, if they pulled someone aside on their own then they could probably have a decent chat with them.*
> *Y: But if they just embarrass you ...*

*X: If they stand you out the front of the class right and take the piss out of you, then you're going to turn round and say something you're going to regret to them.* **(Cardiff)**

*They know you are going to argue. Teachers shouldn't shout, it makes you feel stupid … They would embarrass me and shout at me at school, say I was stupid. I had to rebel, otherwise I'd feel stupid.* **Janine (Camberwell)**

*The teachers can be really, really aggressive, like you know they like to ask questions about your family background and yourself and you wouldn't like to say, and you wouldn't like to be really rude to them. You like to put everything you know because they are holding you and you want to do what they tell you to do and you have to do it because you're young and because you're in school you have to do it.* **Pamela (Oxford)**

*Oh, I think they sort of pushed the ones that were, you know, excelling. Pushed them in all honesty to see if they could break them. It's like, "We don't want you to succeed, so we're going to break you so you have no interest" … The teachers were no good at it. They were no good at being teachers, or they just didn't have no policies, so they'd be able to see for themselves what the school wanted to achieve … They just had to show up and they're getting paid and their six-week holiday, or whatever, a year.* **(Derry)**

*You know when a teacher used to tell me what to do, I still wouldn't understand it and I'd say, "Miss, I don't understand it", and she'd say, "You're just being stupid, get on with your fucking work."* **Emily (Hull)**

Others were more sympathetic to their teachers.

*The thing with teachers is, I mean this school is a good school, I mean one of the best in Scotland but schools nowadays, classes are getting bigger and bigger and teachers are finding it harder to cope with so many pupils and they're only giving attention to the ones that are doing the work, their homework. Anyone else who is not doing it to the standard that the teacher wants is just left.* **G (Aberdeenshire)**

*Teachers are human beings at the end of the day. They are somebody's dad, somebody's brother, somebody's sister.* **Christine**

*When I started school there was this teacher and I hated her. Then when I went into care she totally changed and she's now my best friend and always will be. She is the only person I can ever talk to and trust. And she's a teacher.* **Zoe**

*Inside the classroom one teacher was a complete arsehole and then in drama when you get to know them they are fine, they relax. When they are being teachers they are different.* **Jen (all Durham)**

And a few regarded their teachers as effective, if brutal.

> *What I remember, yes. Sent to the principal's office one day for doing nothing. Literally like, nothing in the class, just sitting there. I probably had a pen in my hand, but only picked up wee bits and pieces – I didn't understand. "Why are you not doing your work? What are you doing?", "Nothing." "Call the principal, go tell the principal you were sent down for doing nothing." He sat me down, gave me a big lecture. I came out of the place crying. Left me in tears – he was good at reducing people. He probably didn't like being reduced himself. So in that sense [school] was good. It was all good boys basically. If you wanted to learn you could.* **(Derry)**

Specific teachers, both good and bad, made strong impressions on the young people, as this discussion from the group in Edinburgh demonstrates.

> *I used to work for my maths teacher because he used to be a laugh and you could have a conversation with him. You liked him because he respected you as well.*

> *At [school], teachers just didn't survive. They used to feed us all the student teachers.*

> *If it was just rote learning it was so boring and people just lost interest.*

> *The drama teacher in our school was brilliant. She was just so into it and used to do really good shows.*

> *Our guidance teacher used to say, "If you ever have problems come and see me." He was also the assistant head teacher of chemistry. He had no time for chemistry or guidance. I remember once this lassie kept following me about and I went to see him and said it was personal and he said he was sorry he couldn't do anything about it. He said, "If it's personal go and talk to your dad" and I said, "I don't have one" and he says, "Do you have an uncle?" and I said, "Oh, he's an arsehole as well." So I just told him, "There's this lassie and she keeps following me about" and he said, "Why don't you do your usual ... take her, use her, abuse her and get rid of her." And that was my guidance teacher and I always remember that to this day.* **(Edinburgh)**

## Bullying

Many young people complained about bullying at school, though one admitted,

> *I always feel guilty hearing about people getting bullied in school cos I was a bully. The thing is right, in my school, you had to either be a bully or be bullied. You couldn't just go to that school and just sail through.* **(Edinburgh)**

Others found it a major barrier to learning.

*But one of the reasons you find school boring is bullying, cos people pick on you all the time, so you find yourself really low and you resist it and you don't want to learn anything because you will be thinking, if I say anything now people will pick on me. For example, I don't understand things and I want to ask questions but people say, "Oh shut up, you don't understand it." It's not as if they understand it but they don't want anyone to ask the question again. I feel really scared sometimes if I'm going to talk and they put me down actually that I can't even ask questions.* **Pamela (Oxford)**

A young Traveller explained that bullying had put her off going to secondary school.

*I didn't like going to secondary school and mammy didn't really like me going either – well she wanted me to go but I didn't want to go. I thought I might get beaten up in the bathrooms.* **S (Belfast)**

Most young people were unclear about what could be done about bullying, though some suggested bullying councils, where other pupils dealt with the problems rather than teachers. Some who had been victims of bullying felt they had been let down by their teachers.

*See the bullies at school. Do you remember being told, "If you're being bullied you should tell us, nobody will find out". Well, it got to the stage where lunch was getting stolen and things like that. Eventually I told my mum and she came to see the guidance teacher. The day after that I went up to the shop at lunchtime and I got two black eyes. Not only that, they were suspended for bullying me. I'll never trust teachers again. Everyone knew I had been the one who had told about it. Everyone knows there is bullying in schools and there is now a campaign out about it. But it won't get any better if people can't trust the teachers.* **(Edinburgh)**

In addition to classic bullying, violence between pupils and, in some cases, from teachers was also a problem for some young people.

*Yeah, because you end up fighting in school, like for instance there is always riots between St Mellons and Lane Rhymney. Can't say that though cos I'm from Rhymney myself, yeah, but it is always people going wrong from St Mellons, but that all the younger ones, yeah, well at the end of the day they are the ones that are like not going to end up getting their GCSEs.* **(Cardiff)**

*But it was full on violent as well. There were people suspended every week for stabbing. There were teachers suspended for battering pupils, pupils suspended for battering teachers. The head used to publicly smash people. I think because my brother used to always bash me too, you learnt very quickly the system was shit and if you weren't going to be like that you may as well just do what you want and not let it get to you. I just learnt how to drift, to avoid the hassles.* **(Edinburgh)**

Many had been involved in fighting and a minority had committed violent offences themselves.

*Interviewer: What did you get expelled for?*
*X: Stabbing the teacher in the shoulder with a screwdriver. (Hull)*

Drugs were widely available in most schools and for some young people, it was where they first became involved in drug use.

*The school was in the paper too. The headmaster went and accused all the guys of being drug dealers and all the lassies of being prostitutes. I did get done for cannabis at the time. My girlfriend at the time was also charged with prostitution because we were caught shagging behind the sheds and the CID went and caught us and they had seen me hand over money to her earlier. But I was just loaning her money and they had recorded a conversation between us when I gave her a tenner. One or two were prostitutes but nothing like what they made out. People always dealt in territories. Mine was in vallies. But we never let hard drugs get into the school. Just cannabis. We actually stopped a lot of people getting into drugs cos dealers were always trying to get into the school. You could get an oxo cube and microwave it and sell it as hash. It was really funny.*

*I was a bigger alkie up to the age of sixteen than I have ever been since. We used to just get stoned every day to cope. Used to go to school to see what you could get. People did a lot of gas. It was a complete survival tool and it was cheap. Everyone knew it was just something to do to pass the time. (Edinburgh)*

## Truanting and school exclusions

Truanting and exclusion from school, both temporary and permanent, have been rising for several years. In 1993–94, government research found that permanent exclusions had risen to over 11,000, a year in and in 1997, the figure was 12,700. There is no centrally collected data on temporary exclusions or suspensions, but it has been estimated that some 135,000 take place each year. Young people in the Real Deal consultation reported that, among other forms of punishment, suspension was often used. For some, it was the start of their exclusion from education.

*X: I think I was fairly suspended at one time, but they only suspended me for a week. I stayed out of school for three months and no one came looking for me. And that was me then, in terms of education.*
*Interviewer: And was there no attempt made to get you back into school, into some kind of education?*
*X: No and that was the end of me and school. When I did go back, I enjoyed the crack, but that's all. I went in but I'd left school really. (Derry)*

*I didn't leave because I wanted to leave. I didn't want to leave because the school was shite, because the school was spot on, you got to wear your own jeans, you got to wear your own clothes.... I had nowhere to go. K Academy even refused me and that is very bad because they take everybody, even expelled folk. I got a private tutor. He was just a waste of time. The only thing he taught me was drink driving at the age of fifteen ... He was just fine, he would get paid by the government for doing nothing at all. I just told him to fuck off.* **T (Aberdeenshire)**

For many, the traumas they were facing at home made them unable to focus on going to school. This was raised in discussions on counselling and support services, which many young people argued should be better and more easily available. Here, the Hull group discusses some of the reasons why regular school attendance can be difficult.

> *Interviewer: Anything else?*
> *Q: Problems at home. That's why I didn't go to school.*
> *Interviewer: Problems at home?*
> *Q: Yeah, being a young carer. Having responsibility for me mam and me sister.*
> *Skezz: Well, at home you could get beat up by your dad and not want to go to school.*
> *Interviewer: What, they don't go to school because they've got bruises on them?*
> *Skezz: Yeah.*
> *Interviewer: And is that cos they don't want to go to school or because their parents won't let them go?*
> *Skezz: Cos if you go to school with bruises on your arm the kids will notice.*

For the minority of young people who had experience of post-school education, it was generally an improvement.

> *Further education is much better cos you can choose what you want to do and you are sorted out and you want to learn it and get something from it.* **(Edinburgh)**

> *That's what it's like at college, just T-shirts and jeans for everyone, it's first names, everyone swears, everyone talks about getting pissed on Friday night and no one cares. But there is still a little bit of discipline cos you still need to get the work done. At the end of the day though the teachers get paid whether or not you get the work done so it's up to you.* **Marzy (Durham)**

Given the importance of parental influence on attitudes to both education and work, the young people were asked what sources of information they had used in making various choices about their education. Although some young people said they had been responsible for all their decisions, most felt their parents had been a major influence.

> *I think your parents have got a lot to do with it anyway because if you think you are going to get put on report you think shit, I've got to tell me mam and dad. I know I thought if I don't get a good education I can't mess me dad about and not get a job. He always used to tell me, "If you don't get a good education you'll end up washing tables*

*and floors for the rest of your life." So in the last two years I thought, shit, I'm really going to have to get my head together.* **Zoe (Durham)**

*I got loads of pressure, especially from my dad. He wanted me to go into psychology, go into his business, [and] said, "I'll support you to do this." They never encouraged me to do what I wanted to do.* **Courtney (Buffy House)**

*You know when you have one of those open days? And you have to show your parents all your work and stuff – I did this wicked art stuff – it's still in my bedroom, it's that good. And my dad was saying, "Yes, it's dead brilliant", and the art teacher was saying, "Yeah, she's brilliant, brilliant." But then my dad was saying, "But hang on, how long is it going to take her to earn that money?" So he told me what I was going to do, business-wise.* **(Camberwell)**

Others felt their parents were uninterested in their education.

*Some parents just don't care. They could be alcoholics, junkies … My parents didn't care. They left it up to me.* **Steve (Camberwell)**

Though most young people said their parents did want them to go to school and were keen for them to 'get an education', they also felt that parents had little influence over them after a certain age, particularly regarding school attendance.

*And this stuff about taking your parents to court if you don't go to school. That should be abolished as well cos it's not fair that they get fined if they can't make their kids go to school. All the parents I know are trying their hardest to make their kids go … well, my dad didn't do well at school and he said that's why he wants me to do well. I think that's one of the biggest things that makes parent want you to do well is like if they haven't done well.* **Hoysey (Hull)**

Others felt that while their parents had encouraged them to go to school, it had sometimes been counterproductive.

*If they're always shouting at you to go you're going to not go if you're in that rebellious stage. It's like that thing with drugs, you're not supposed to tell them not to do it, just help them to get off it.* **Hoysey (Hull)**

*All the kids that I know, all their fucking mothers and fathers, they're all wanting them to go to school, trying to make 'em go to school. You know my mam, right, she used to do everything to make me go to school. She used to try locking me up until 9 o'clock and then take me brother.* **Chris (Hull)**

Some felt that the government stress on parental responsibility for school attendance was misplaced.

*Hoysey: I think the reason for the government blaming parents is to shift the blame off them. Because the education people are supposed to be making education more interesting and they're just shifting the blame.*
*Q: If they did a bit more research about what was going on in our heads they would know what else to do instead, if they cared a bit more.* **(Hull)**

## Lifelong learning

Lifelong learning was a difficult idea for most of the young people to grasp. While many recognised that the world of work would require further training, many of those who had had bad experiences in school were unenthusiastic about further learning. They recognised that learning took place in a range of environments, though for some these environments were somewhat risky.

*Interviewer: Where else have you learnt things?*
*Hoysey: At home, your family. At football, at rugby.*
*Q: Telly.*
*Skezz: Friends.*
*Interviewer: What do you learn from friends?*
*Skezz: Stuff you get up to on a night time, causing mischief, like last night, someone got their hand blown off by a firework.*
*Bart: Prison ... you learn card tricks, anything you want to. Yeah, go to Moorlands and you can do hairdressing and mechanics and everything. They've got a proper salon in Moorlands where you can go and get your nails clipped and your hair dyed and stuff.*
*Anna: What do you learn at home then?*
*Q: How to cope with your mam.*
*Skezz: How to be quiet.*
*Hoysey: How to be sociable.*
*Q: How to watch Family Fortunes without falling asleep!*
*Skezz: Learning at work.*
*Anna: What do you learn at work?*
*Skezz: Learning how to make pizzas, learning how to take orders on the phone, learning how to serve. Learning all different things.*
*Anna: So what do you learn with your mates apart from illegal stuff?*
*Hoysey: You learn about friendship and about what proper friendship is.* **(Hull)**

Despite, or perhaps because of, the risks, some of the young people felt they had learnt more useful skills outside school than in it. As Emily from the Hull group explained, 'Do you know if I went to school I wouldn't be as streetwise as I am now. I'd rather be streetwise.' This was echoed more graphically by a young person in Cardiff, 'GCSE help you survive on the street? No, a six-inch blade does.'

## Leaving school

Given the fact that for many of these young people, school attendance is, at best, partial after adolescence, the notion of 'leaving school' as an important marker in life was missing. Unlike their parents' or grandparents' generation, secure employment was not available to them. Whole industries such as steel, mining and shipbuilding have simply disappeared, a fact with which many of the young people were all too familiar.

> X: *If you haven't got a really good education [nowadays] like gone to university, or whatever, it's harder to get a job.*
> Y: *In my father's time, 10,000 people were employed in steelworks.*
> X: *But then my father, he came out of high school and he was straight into a job, but like nowadays you come out of high school and you've really got to search for a job.*
> *(Cardiff)*

> Marzy: *When me dad was my age he was working in the pit and I couldn't do that cos there are no pits any more.*
> John: *My dad said that when he was young if he got sick of a job at one factory he could turn around and say, "Hey, I'm off" and walk into the next factory and get a job.*
> Chunk: *Back in the 1950s you could leave school on a Friday and start work on the Saturday.*
> Lisa: *Me mum had to grow up fast cos she left school, got a job and was married when she was seventeen.*
> Marzy: *When me dad started working at the pit his dad treat him like an adult and said, "Oh, now you're a man".* *(all Durham)*

This was in sharp contrast to the experience of signing on and other dealings with the welfare system.

> *Careers and social services and dole – fill this form in, bring it back next week. And social services do treat you like kids cos they don't let you make your own decisions.*
> *Emily (Hull)*

## Improving experience of education

Despite their disenchantment with the formal education they had received the young people were full of ideas on how things could be improved. These included improving teacher training, more practical and 'real life' skills on the curriculum and improved counselling services.

> *Teachers should have to work with young people. Their training just seems to teach them about the subject, but not how to talk to young people.*

> *I think teachers should have to do some kind of work in the communities around them first. They just don't have a clue what is happening around them in some of these areas.*
> *(Edinburgh)*

Many felt that school counselling services, if they existed at all, were inadequate for their needs. They wanted one person, who was not a teacher, to whom personal problems could be taken. For many, the problems they were having in their personal lives interfered with, even obliterated, their chances of educational progress, a fact that they felt had not been picked up in the education system.

*I think there needs to be a counsellor in schools. Someone who is not a teacher of any subject but can be trusted.*

*They need to be someone over twenty who understands young people. They need to be old enough to have some experience, but not a Victorian.*

*I hated the fact that I had to explain to every single teacher why I was missing class and I just expected to tell one confidentially.*

*A child psychologist used to see me once a week for an hour and that was all good and well, but I was left to deal with all that shit on my own and it really screwed me up. I just couldn't get it out. All it was doing was bringing it to the surface so I had to find a way to get it out myself. Since I wasn't very good at talking about it, it was just anger. And that was my way.*

*See if you knew they were really listening and you thought they would try to help, then you felt a lot better. Everybody should have a right to be able to talk to someone.* **(Edinburgh)**

Many felt that a broader range of subjects, particularly 'life skills', should be taught and that this would help make schooling more relevant to the lives of young people. The idea of peer educators or other non-teachers going back into schools to explain life skills was also suggested.

*X: I really think they should teach people "If you are unemployed, if you are homeless this is what you need to do".*
*Y: This is about basic survival and if they don't teach you that at school, who cares about bloody history? There just isn't a back-up system if all the others like family and that fail before you get a chance.*
*Z: They show you how to shag at school; they should show you how to fill up dole forms.*
*Y: I didn't get any sex education anyway.*
*X: I think they should have people who have been through it going into schools and saying, "This is what happened to me and this is what I did." ***(Edinburgh)**

*Alcohol awareness.* **John**

*They don't give you drugs awareness until it's too late, until Year 11 when they say, "This is cannabis" and we all say, "Yeah, we know."* **Jen**

*Budgeting, you don't really get to know about that.* **Tanya (all Durham)**

*I really think there needs to be much more in school – choices about subjects and sex and social education and stuff about drugs and that.*

*I think there should be a choices period every week where you can go and talk to someone if you want to or find out about other things like jobs and training.*

*There should be some kind of supported study rather than just homework. Then you could help when you need it to do things and learn more.*

*I think basically that fourteen to sixteen are really bad ages to learn anything and that more time needs to be spent on learning about life and all that. You are more able to learn subjects and focus on it later.* **(Edinburgh)**

*I didn't like history because there was no black history, only cotton fields. They told us about the Saxons and the Romans.* **Deborah (Camberwell)**

The relevance of some lessons on issues such as drugs and sex was also questioned as the pupils often felt they knew more than the teachers.

*We got sex education and drugs and alcohol but we got on to the drugs subject then people like me started saying that's a heap of shite and the teachers just said cut it, you ken more than me, we don't want to show that you know more than me.*
**T (Aberdeenshire)**

The London groups felt discipline could be improved through the use of disciplinary boards made up of teachers, student representatives, parents and some independent people. It was felt these would give students a 'fair hearing'.

*I think there should be a disciplinary committee including your school mates because they know more about your problems.* **Keith**

*There should be a board of student representatives, teachers, parents and independent people.* **Winifred**

*Independent people are the best route. Parents might just want what is best for the school … I've been there, suspended three times because the parents wanted the rubbish out.*
**Janine (all Camberwell)**

Other young people were more fatalistic about discipline.

**Interviewer:** *All right, well, what should be done about bad behaviour then?*
*X: There's nothing you can do.*
*Y: Everyone wants to have a laugh though in school, isn't it, everyone does.*
*Z: But for some reason each generation just seems to be getting worse and worse.*

*Interviewer: Because the rules …*

*X: Because the discipline and that are going down.*

*Y: Like other people, other people's role models.*

*Z: Need to be more up to date.*

*Y: But like as you said as the generation goes down there's bound to be a fault some-where along the line, isn't it, because someone obviously not looked up to someone else and decided to do it their own way, disciplinary action is disintegrating.* **(Cardiff)**

*Budgie: Maybe if we had gone to Trinity House [naval school] we wouldn't be here now, ending up how we are.*

*Stu: Why wouldn't we? Look at Y – he went to Trinity House and he's a fuckin' smack-head.*

*A: It's got nothing to do with school, how you turn out.*

*Craig: What's it got to do with then?*

*Budgie: Discipline.* **(Hull)**

*Lisa: I wouldn't have minded getting the cane when I was at school cos it would have knocked me into line.*

*Chunk: Christ, if they had caned us, I would be dead. I would be six foot under.*

*Zoe: If I got hit over the hand once, I would be so shit scared to ever do it again.* **(Durham)**

Though other forms of punishment were also seen as questionable in their effectiveness.

*Punishment exercises are totally pointless and they just used to piss you off.*

*Ours had three stages – one you had to do by yourself, two had to be signed by your par-ents, and three they called your parents into the school.*

*I used to hold five pencils at once and do five lines at a time.* **(Edinburgh)**

And some young people felt that the timing of education was wrong and perhaps should be more fluid.

*Maybe you could have your school life split up into four rather than three so that when you're eight you go to a different school and you're more prepared for it and you might get to know what you want more. When you go to senior school you get all your options and course work flung at you – it could be done more gradually.* **Zoe (Durham)**

This was especially true for exams. Some of those who had taken them felt were too clustered together and pressurised.

*When I had my exams they were too close to each other, I had one every day, I think they should space the exams out more so you can have a rest between exams. Cos if you're doing an exam every day it just burns you out. You're supposed to learn for your exams and I had six exams in six days which is a lot of work.* **Hoysey (Hull)**

### Barriers to education

Several other issues were raised as barriers to education. These included money, particularly for further and higher education and the care of children. The replacement of grants by loans did not meet approval from the young people in the Real Deal. Some feared it would prevent them going on to further study and reinforce social divisions in higher education,

*If you are claiming income support and are living in a flat on your own you can't have a grant. I think that should be totally the other way around, if you are living on your own you can't afford to pay for all your bus fares. It used to cost me a fortune to buy all my own books and my dinner when I was there and bit and pieces.* **Zoe**

*I hate the idea of being in debt and I just wouldn't do it.* **Marzy**

*How do they expect people to become doctors and stuff like that where it takes years and years, living on a loan? And we need doctors, they are essential people. Everybody has a place and a role in society, and if it's going to cost people to be good people and decent people then people will turn more to crime, won't they.* **Christine**

*It's going to be like the old days when people who are rich have a better education than those who can't afford it. It will divide the classes.* **Lisa (all Durham)**

*Like, if you want a really good job, you've got to go to university, and you have got to have money to start off. So if you haven't got money as a basis to start off, then you are not going to be able to get better pay.* **(Cardiff)**

For a minority of the young people, responsibilities for childcare were an active barrier.

*Well, it's not just that, you go on to college you need money to get by and all that you can't go to college and keep a part-time job up or something like that, cos that's hard enough. You need to get out and get a job now. I've got an eight month old baby and it's hard enough looking after him as it is.* **(Cardiff)**

*The thing is because I want to go to college and then university I need help with childcare and travel expenses. I really want to do a degree. I'd need to find somewhere with a crèche.*

*Everyone keeps saying "education, education, education" and I want to go for it but I can't because of the childcare.*

*I know people in the past who went to uni and they got grants they could live on, they got housing benefit and they could get the dole during the summer holidays if they couldn't find a job. Now it's so hard because you know even if you get a grant it won't be enough and you'll have to go into debt.* **(Edinburgh)**

## One to one findings

Many of the views brought out in group discussions were reinforced by the young people interviewed one to one. Among them, there were two main views of education; either education was 'worthless' and unable to affect a person's chance of getting on in life, or it was vital. Those who considered it worthless argued that 'It's only a piece of paper at the end of the day' and professed more faith in an education of life and common sense. Ability, it was suggested, was in the doing rather than the theory. The people who felt this way tended to be those who had left school early or those with few qualifications. Others felt that having qualifications had not helped them into a job.

*Because I don't see me doing another four years doing maths or Latin is going to help me in life. I'm getting by just now, and I got, I passed my standard grades at school when I was fifteen and never been back.* **Bill, Scottish, 20, London**

The second, and slightly more common, view was that education was essential. 'Without them [English and maths] you can't get nowhere.' Some young people were very ambitious in their educational goals and had applied for courses to help them attain their ambitions. Those holding these views were more likely to have some experience of further education and to know what was available. For some, education was important to help them back to independence. Another view was that 'it gave you an aim in life'.

*Getting an education is very, very important to me. I came out of university when my mother was ill so now I am trying to get back into there. It is good to achieve by yourself, so this is my, you know, start picking up the pieces … to get my education is very important. If I go back and get my degree and after that do my masters and hopefully God willing do my PhD.* **Tim, Black, 24, London**

Others, however, felt that it was 'too late' for them to learn. Despite regretting not having achieved much at school, they felt this was irreversible and their concern was to get on without qualifications. Others felt unable to think about education, arguing that their immediate aim was to find a home.

*Yes, I wish I could go back [to school], but it's too late. For me it is anyway, I don't want to. I mean everyone is saying to me, yeah, if I could go back a couple of years then I would have done it, but it's too late, I'm in that stage where I want to make money, I don't want to be going to college waiting round getting little Giros, I want to be making some money and I mean every week.* **Mark, 20, London**

## Barriers to education

Barriers to education centred around money and motivation. Some of the young people had been studying for degrees and had dropped out because of their financial situation. This was most common among those who had made it to university but had no parental support. Having not finished their degree they felt they were now in a 'trap' of being over-qualified but unable to complete an academic qualification.

> *I've got As, got maths, physics, chemistry, German, got four A levels at A and two ASs at A and B so I'm not stupid, but that's got me out of jobs because people are like "Why aren't you going to university?" I say I can't go to university because I haven't got any money because the government has just taken the grants off and they've made it impossible for anybody to go to university or anybody without parental support to go to university … You know, I got to university, and after three weeks I didn't have any money, no money, no prospects. They were going to kick me out, kick me out at the end of the term and then me go and be homeless over Christmas … I didn't feel I should have been at university because I hadn't had the charmed upbringing that everybody else had.* **Ruby, White European, 20, London**

Others had looked into courses and had been prevented from undertaking them because of the cost. One suggestion was that young people should be paid for staying on in education.

> *It's very, very expensive being in art college. They give you a grant of about £560 for the year. On top of that, and I know from being in art college once before, I spent three months in art college and spent £200 on art equipment alone. There's only about nine and a half months in an academic year, so I did just under a third and spent £200, which is over the £560 mark, isn't it? Then after all of that, because being in college you're not allowed on the Giro, which means I've got to find other funding for things like food.* **Marcus, White, 20, London**

> *The one thing that put me off my education was you don't get paid for it. I mean I worked for a year for £29.50, but that was only because I had to stay in education. So I left school early, I had to do another year and I was doing the same work as another mechanic but he was getting paid about £180 at the end of the week and I was getting £29.50. They could do a lot better than that, like college grants and university grants.* **Bill, Scottish, 20, London**

A second barrier was a lack of emotional support. Many felt that to succeed in education it was important to be motivated, 'to have a goal' and 'a focal point in mind about what you want to do'. For this, they needed encouragement. Similarly some felt that they were liable to be 'impatient and badly behaved' in a class situation and needed support to get them through.

> *The only help I need is motivation and to have someone to push me to it, or I'll go back down again.* **Paul, White, 19, London**

*So I need support, someone like pushing me because sometimes I'm quite lazy, pushing me to do what I want to do, and going to university and getting a job and whatever.* **Lynda, African, 20, London**

### Improving experiences of education

As in the consultation groups, a common criticism was that education did not prepare people for life and, in particular, how to survive away from home and out of the educational system. Drawing on their own experiences, some pointed out that they had been ignorant when they left home about what homelessness meant in practical terms and what help was available to them. Some suggested that schools should teach people their 'rights and how to contact services'. Others wanted young people in school to be warned about homelessness and other problems such as drug addiction, possibly through visits by ex-homeless people or drug users.

*Show them videos and that. Not to shock them but ... to shock them as well like, but show them videos and pictures of people or take people around like who can say that I am an ex heroin addict, you know what I mean. This is what it is like. Show them examples.* **Tom, White Scottish, 24, London**

*I'd put for normal families, the school and stuff, I'd make sure that there was plenty of school counsellors around. Even if you can't afford counsellors, get some of the older students to volunteer, or students from colleges – something like that. You'd be surprised how many people are willing to volunteer and help for nothing. Especially young people at school and colleges, they don't have much to do in their free time anyway, apart from work.* **Nazeema, Asian, 16, London**

Another suggestion was that vocational courses could be taught at a younger age. Academic education, it was felt, was not suitable for all people. One person explained that doing something practical sooner might have helped him stay out of trouble.

# Working

## Findings

The Real Deal participants have a range of work experiences. Some are currently employed either full or part-time and many of those in education work part-time and at weekends. Most have also worked at some time in the informal and illegal economies. Some of those still in full-time education and those who are unemployed had little exposure to formal work. For the majority, the labour market had been a difficult and unsatisfactory experience, often because of the cycle of poor qualifications and low pay. Many felt distant and disengaged from the world of work.

Many had also worked, sometimes as volunteers, in the youth clubs or venues where the discussions took place. Some reported a desire to carry on working with other young people. At least two of the groups in the project, the Nucleus in Derry and Tangents in Edinburgh, included some peer educators. As one young person in Derry explained, 'It's the ideal setting for me to do the kind of work I want to do. It's the sort of place you designed in your head when you were young.'

Most participants were well aware of the increasing need for qualifications to gain secure work, though the increasing cost of higher education was noted by some as a barrier. Given their general lack of qualifications, the discussion of work was dominated by the problems of low pay and insecurity. Jobs included bar work, fast food and pizza parlours, shops, paper rounds, cleaning and, in some cases, factory work. Some had worked on commission-only jobs, cold calling or 'canvassing'. The following story is typical.

> *I was still at school and I'd had my first discussion with my mum telling her that I was leaving and that I had enough and that all my friends had left and she said well you are not leaving school until you have got a job, so I had to go and find a job. So we were in the Job Centre and the baker were looking for someone so I tried there. And the woman gave me an interview so I was told to turn up at 9 o'clock on Monday morning for a week's trial and I thought rare, a bakery, cakes and pies, good. So I turned up and I told my teachers at school I was going on a week's trial and they said best of luck. I turned up, saw the woman I was supposed to see, that was fine, I got a uniform. The first job I had to do was to take Sunblest bread and put it in to bags and seal it up and scrape chip pans and working me hard and keeping my head down and doing as best I could. There was never any mention of wages or anything like this so I went up to the office, it was about 4 o'clock. I done a lot of sweeping of the floor, the flour on the floor, I went up to the office, the pay was something like £1.67 an hour, so I was just getting £12 a day. There was no way I was working for just over sixty quid a week. The woman said like I was lucky to have this job and I said well send my cheque in the post and left my address and I got a cheque for £11.57 or something ... That was my first and worst experience.*

Another young person, from the Edinburgh group, described their working life so far.

> *After leaving school, roughly I didn't work for a year, because my housing officer told me I couldn't afford to live in the hostel if I had a job, so, no work for a year. I moved into Aberdeen and did a bit of temping, cleaning toilets and waiting and all that sort of thing. It was £4 an hour, which was better than you get doing most things. Then I went on to sell windows which is great fun. You can get £60 for an hour's work – it just gets cold in the winter. I gave up with that. I went on to Camphill Community for a couple of months, which was fine, apart from it got too stressful. You were waking up to get everyone ready at 7 o'clock in the morning – Camphill is a community working with people with learning difficulties and mental illness, supposedly working as equals and everything running like a commune. But you're getting everyone ready at 7 o'clock in the morning and you weren't finishing until 11pm. And then you were running into the pub for last orders two miles away and then wandering back again. I stuck that out for a short while – not long enough – got back to [a rural area] and they put me on £15 a week because I was living with my parents again and I had actually been working so I*

*didn't qualify for this £15 a week even though I was under eighteen. But they took me off that and put me on a YTS. Apart from my interview with the woman, she took one look at my CV and said I've got nothing for you, you're under-qualified and over-experienced. So she stuck me in college doing textiles. Which was great. I learned how to use a knitting machine if you ever want anything knitted. It was great because in the end I learnt how to use them just as well as the tutors. But I never really turned up. There was no reason to. I still got paid whether I turned up or not. And then the tutor needed some help doing computing – in fact she couldn't use the computer – so I went up and showed everyone how to use the computers which was fine, except surely they should employ a proper computing lecturer rather than getting some YTS to do it? That ended and I hung about for a while then I went to the fish factory. Now that was a good one. £300 a week for working four nights a week, 10pm to 6am, sometimes 8am, it was roughly 40 hours guaranteed. Even if they only wanted you in for ten hours that week, you still got paid for 40. I could pay my rent no bother, come down here if I wanted with my wages and not worry about it, I still had enough money to pay my rent. But that ended, it was Christmas work. And not many places guarantee you 40 hours anyway. From there – my best one – my next job after that, I came down here I was going to travel round Britain for a while so while visiting my mother I went into the job centre to keep her happy and I ended up with a job. It was the first time I had ever gone into a job centre and they have given me a job. It's not something that connects.*

*Y: You go in there to get lectured and told you're not getting any work.*
*Interviewer: So what did you get?*
*Y: Barmaid. At this lovely little Italian restaurant which ended up to be absolute hell. By the time I got the sack, I was working at weekends, I was working 9am to 3am and still expected to come in at 9am the next morning although if I was lucky I could sneak maybe half an hour lunch break, which I'd usually go the pub around the corner and have a couple of drinks to keep me calm. I was answering telephones, doing bookings, preparing desserts, doing drinks, coffees, helping out front, doing waitressing, helping out in the kitchen if they needed that, helping out downstairs whatever – for £3.20 an hour. I'm still trying to figure out "why?" I actually got the sack. I was working on the Friday night, I was working from 9am till 3am and I actually got hit on the back of the head with a full bottle of Chianti. It was an accident but a full bottle of Chianti on the back of the head is sore. I went to casualty, waited until 4.30 to be seen, got sent home and was expected to turn up for work at 9 o'clock the next morning. I was rather foul tempered at work the next day and I had the Monday off, thank goodness. I went back on the Tuesday and I had a really bad day because I'd been out the night before and my boss's best mate landed on my doorstep when I was ill and my mother let him in. He decided he was staying with me that night so I was in a severely foul mood when I got in the next day and I got the sack for having a bad attitude. So I got sacked at 1 o'clock in the morning. Then I got fed up and I just did one end of Union Street to the other. I only got halfway up Union Street and got offered three jobs, the best of which was a trainee bar manageress with a view to me becoming bar manageress six months later. I*

*did a week and a half of that and found out I was pregnant and freaked out. And that's my working life.*

Complaints about low pay and not being given the rate of pay advertised were common.

*Dunny: After college I started working doing canvassing [double-glazing].*
*Interviewer: And that didn't work out, did it?*
*Dunny: I was there ten weeks.*
*Interviewer: Why did you leave?*
*Dunny: Because they ripped me off.*
*Bart: Gave him a £10 pay slip and they didn't even pay me – that's why I fucked it off.*
*Dunny: Gave me a £10 pay slip and it should have been like £350.*
*Bart: None of them paid me. Oh, yeah, I got one payslip and that was for £21, and your basics cost you £60.*
*Interviewer: How much did they advertise you'd get?*
*Dunny: Oh, it's like you're self-employed.*
*Hoysey: I only worked at [a window company] three weeks. The basic was only on for the first three weeks ... £80 a week. I left after that.*
*Interviewer: Do you know other young people who had a similar experience?*
*Dunny: Well, Bart had the same. He got ripped off.*
*Bart: I didn't even get paid, did I? Worked a week and they didn't even pay me.* **(Hull)**

*[Burger chain] is £3.65 an hour – it was absolutely shite. Although if you did overtime it went up to £5.50. I did a whole week – a whole week of fourteen-hour shifts and it absolutely killed me. And the heat you have to work under because they don't have air conditioning. It's so, so busy and it doesn't have any air conditioning and I collapsed three times in there in the space of a week. That was the worst job I ever had and I'll never ever go back to it.*

*I haven't had many jobs and the ones I have [had] have been pretty crap, like training schemes, and I've been sacked for being rude to my boss or to customers. I got sacked for being rude to old women in a café who came in and sat all day and drank cups of tea and doing nothing else and giving me cheek and dirty looks so I started giving quite subtle hints, but my boss picked up on me saying things and I got turfed out. And that's the way it went everywhere else. I think it's crap money – you're put on training schemes and expected to work nine to five and somebody next to you can be earning a £100 plus a week and you get £35 a week. It's exploitation, so I used to just refuse and the careers office stopped my money so many times at the job centre because I used to argue with them. "Why don't you go to college?" [they asked]. I said, "I don't want to go to college." "Oh well, we'll stop your money then." And then they used to force you into going to college and when you're there then they say, "Only go when it's right for you." I used to get so frustrated because you don't know what to do. They are telling you to do this and then do that and expect you to either pick a training scheme or college course as soon as you leave and if you don't do it then they stop your money.* **(Edinburgh)**

Other had experienced bullying or violence at work, either as victims or participants.

*I had to get up at 5 o'clock in the morning, go to work, stand in line, at the very end of the line, you know these trays you get? You had to count three biscuits out of this tub, round ones and put them into round spaces and I was right at the end, so there were no spaces left. And there was someone in front of me showing me what to do, so I just stood there for an hour and a half, putting them in slowly and then she started shouting at me because I didn't carry enough cardboard boxes downstairs, so I left. It was horrible.*

*I had just come back from my days off … it was the Tuesday, I was off from the Sunday night. I got there about twenty past nine. I went through, got changed, came back in. I was going to make a cup of tea. I was dragged to the big walk-in fridge by the supervisor. She started going on about these little fillets of lamb, right … I would say they would be about four quid in cost altogether. Started going on about them being on a shelf on the Sunday and they are not there now. And I was saying like, it was my day off, I don't know what the fuck you are speaking. And she kept going on and on. Like, they are not there … they've gone missing. And I say, well, maybe they got cooked by the staff. And then she started to say it in a way as though I had nicked them. They were there on Sunday night when I was off and like they weren't there on the Tuesday morning. She just kept going on and on and on. I was just like standing there in this fridge. And there was like this big shelf in front of me and big cartons of cream, two-litre cartons, about 50 of them … and she just kept going on and on in my ear … shouting at me and swearing at me. So I just like swung a punch. It missed her by that, hit all the cream and it all exploded everywhere … So I just like took off saying, "Stick your job up your arse!" So I left.* **(Aberdeenshire)**

## The informal economy

Most of the young people had worked 'cash in hand' at some time or other. For some, it was the only type of work they had had.

*If you're not claiming benefits then it's no skin off their nose, is it, cos you're not getting benefits anyway. I'm not getting any benefits at all but I can still go about and give lessons on the guitar and do what I do and not pay the tax and no one knows about it.* **(Durham)**

In one group, all the young people said they had worked 'cash in hand'.

*X: That's because the system is shit.*
*Y: The system does teach you how to rip it off and how you're going to make more money.*
*Z: The system does show people how to be criminals.*
*X: It also forces you into the feeling that "I'm getting screwed, so I might as well go and screw someone else."*

*Z: When you're classed as self-employed, it's too much hassle to work out your tax and to declare the fact that you are working. Selling windows, you can make an absolute fortune and that's a lot of tax. All the forms you need to do. Fuck that, just sign on at the same time.* **(Hull)**

Most Real Deal participants felt it was justifiable where money was tight and did not regard untaxed income as 'stealing'.

*Tanya: I suppose it is but a lot of people do it anyway, innit, but they don't think of it as a serious crime.*
*Smithy: Aye, but its still a crime, whether you're fiddling or burgling you can still get in trouble with the police.*
*Tanya: But more people wouldn't call you a criminal for fiddling.*
*X: I haven't got a bank account so how would I do it [pay tax]? I would have to open a bank account and I don't like banks, I don't trust them. I worked in a pub and I did just two hours every morning cleaning the pub and I got £36 at the end of the week so I don't think that was too bad. I also used to work in an Indian restaurant for £10 a night working six hours so it wasn't really brilliant pay.* **(Durham)**

Some young people argued that it was wrong not to pay tax, though this argument was hedged with various qualifications about what taxes were used for.

*In Denmark, it's a nanny state. They look after you from birth to grave. There isn't nearly that much poverty – there are some bits that are dodgy, you have the usual problems with heroin – but it looks after you.*

*If you're willing to pay taxes for a system like that, but we don't live in a system like that and I don't see why I should pay taxes – at the moment anyway.*

*I'm willing to pay taxes if that happens.* **(Edinburgh)**

A small number felt that the money to be earned 'cash in hand' made it difficult to think about working legitimately. One young man in the Edinburgh group admitted.

*I've never actually had a job legally, officially or anything that's attached to work. Which is quite funny in the dole office because I walk in and ... [they say] "So, you've not worked once in your entire life since you turned sixteen?" And I go, "That's right." But I did have a job once, briefly. It was a three-week contract painting and decorating, getting paid a £100 a day which was quite good. Which is a bit unfortunate because it makes me think that my time is worth a lot of money now and when I look at average pay for a job, I'm like, no way.*

For a minority, working illegally meant crime rather than not paying tax. For them accepting low-paid 'legal' work was unappealing after the large sums of money that could be made from running or selling drugs.

> X: *Work for me is pretty strange. You've got the legal work and you've got not so legal work. Legal work is bollocks basically. Some of the jobs I had when I was younger, doing it illegally, I made more in a week that I'd probably make in a month working full time. It's really hard for me to get my head round work, because I still get offered some jobs back home which I could do and make anything between a hundred and a couple of hundred quid a day. Trying to get that in any source of legal work at all is impossible. Back home in Glasgow I still get offered a few wee jobs.*
> Interviewer: *What kind of jobs?*
> *When I was younger I used to sell drugs. Then I stopped selling drugs – I must admit I put my foot down there, I ended up making mistakes and selling drugs to someone who was too young. But I was a bit smacked out of my head at the time, so I started being a runner instead which was picking up the parcels from one place and running through an area to another. It's actually a hell of a lot more dangerous. Selling the drugs is a doddle but carrying big packs of it.*
> Interviewer: *You get more for running than you do for dealing …*
> *It's not only that. People start identifying you as well with a wee brown bag. That's what I had. They started to identify me because I had this luminous green Nike bag … I thought I'd try and blend in being a student, but it never quite worked that way … Then I started doing more illegal drugs because when I was younger, I just didn't have much respect for myself and I just wanted money. I had a bit of a drug problem so I just started battering people, which is quite hilarious really. Well, it's not now.*
> Interviewer: *Did you get paid for it?*
> *Got paid a hell of a lot of money. I was roughly getting £500 a job, depending on what needed to get done. But at the time it didn't bother me. It was me and all my pals were doing it, it wasn't just one person going out and doing it, everyone was doing this. There was 97 per cent unemployment and the other 3 per cent were people whose dad owned a company or something and maybe they were lucky enough to get a job and get out of there. Illegally, I was raking it in.* **(Edinburgh)**

Not only was the money to be made from drugs difficult to forsake, as the same speaker admitted:

> *I just found it hard working. I hate working. Illegally, you don't have to work. You can do as little as possible. I know people who work illegally whose only job is to stand on a corner and look out and they get paid a hell of a lot of money. They probably get paid more just standing there for two hours than the majority of people. The thing about illegal work isn't just the money, it's the buzz you get. You do get a really good adrenaline buzz. That's how I moved on to jobs like being a bouncer. The only reason I became a bouncer was to fight every weekend. I was really violent when I was younger and the hardest thing now is not about getting a job – I can get a job – it's just keeping it. I get*

*bored. No matter what job you do, there's only so much you can take out of it. Then you get bored. Same old routine.*

## The value of work

Given their experiences, it is perhaps not surprising that many Real Deal participants were sceptical about the 'value' of work other than as a way to earn money. In addition, the lack of training available in many unskilled jobs led people to feel that working was not necessarily a way to equip oneself with the skills to get better jobs. The young people often saw government emphasis on work as being largely a result of the desire to reduce the benefits bill rather than anything more high-minded.

> *E: Does that [government emphasis on work] mean all the rich have to get jobs too? Like those with millions of pounds? Should they be working? To make them feel better?*
> **Interviewer:** *It says the government wants to get everyone working.*
> *L: Everyone who is taking money from them.*
> *E: Everyone on benefit!* **(Aberdeenshire)**

Others, however, argued that work was beneficial, both for individuals and society. This attitude was displayed by several of the young refugees in the Oxford group.

> **Pamela:** *Work is important, but it's not just important for the money. If I won the lottery tomorrow, I'd still get a job. You need the routine and something to get up for.*
> **Billy:** *Everyone should work if they are not disabled or they've got no sickness or whatever. Because you've got some people who are working and some people who just sit there.*
> **Tigger:** *Fair enough, but you've got to ensure there is wide range of work, not just office jobs*
> **Mr K:** *I think everyone should work to rely on themselves, not others.* **(Oxford)**

They also felt that the value of work lay in the skills one could acquire.

> *You can't just stay at home and expect that you could be there and from there you could get a better job … getting a job and giving up benefit – you could get a better job – get promoted, you might get a pay rise. You put more effort in.* **Billy (Oxford)**

Unlike their education choices, very few people mentioned their parents as sources of either information or advice on jobs. Information about employment opportunities tended to come from more formal sources such as schools, careers advisers and the Employment Service. However, there was criticism of most of these systems. Many young people felt that, in the case of the Employment Service, in particular, better integration would help. There was a wide range of courses and training opportunities available to young people, but information was scattered and not available in an accessible or coherent form. This also applied to information about work and benefits. Several young people said they wanted more information about in-work benefits.

*It's just giving people more information really, so they know. Otherwise at the moment, I think what happens is that someone takes a job and they don't know until they've taken it how much better off they are going to be or worse off.*
**(Buffy House)**

Very few felt they had been well served by careers advice in school, but others said that they had not taken advantage of the system either.

*I just remember leaving school and being told to go and see this careers adviser. But I never went to her, I just went straight into a job and that was it. I don't think school ever prepared us – I just left when I was fifteen. But if I'd stayed on they might have given me a bit more help. Oh, you did get work experience for a week. I worked in a nursery with disabled children – that was quite good, but you didn't really get to choose what you wanted to do ... it was just, at the end of it there's this job left for you. But it was great, fortunately I loved doing the job that I was given, but I think a lot of people don't get the choice of work that they want to do.* **(Edinburgh)**

Different groups within the consultation had distinctive attitudes to work. Young people with experience of homelessness found entry into the world of work particularly difficult. Many complained about being discriminated against by employers because their address was a hostel. Equally important, however, is the fact that many homeless young people have suffered severe trauma or disruption both prior to, and during, homelessness. They may need intensive support to overcome 'prevocational' needs that may have contributed to their homelessness and will not be met by providing accommodation or skills training. In Buffy House, a high support hostel in London, some of the discussion at that group centred around the young people's anxieties about being pushed too quickly into the workplace.

*That is one thing that they need to get straight is rushing people into work when they are not ready. Especially people like us in a hostel like this. You're only going to make things worse for the person if they end up in a job they don't like. That is one of the reason I ended up here is because of the contract of living at Drury Lane [another Centrepoint hostel] I couldn't cope with it. Couldn't cope with all the demands and hassles, it just sent me spiralling down and back at square one basically.* **Emma**

Other young people found their entry to the world of work difficult because of criminal records.

**Hoysey:** *So if you walk into a place, and they said, "Sorry, we can't employ you because you've been in prison."*
**Bart:** *But they don't say that, they just say, "Oh, we'll let you know."*
**Hoysey:** *Yeah they do, they say, "I'm sorry, you've got a criminal record, we can't employ you."*
**Bart:** *None of them said that to me. They say, "We'll let you know in a couple of weeks" and they don't.*
**Hoysey:** *If you go into a shop and you get a job and say you haven't got a criminal*

*record, and they find out you have, they just lay you off.*
*Bart: That's why honesty comes first.*
*Hoysey: But we're talking about that … and people should be treated as equal no matter what they've done.*
*Interviewer: Bart, so you've experienced people discriminating against you because you've been in prison, but you still don't think it's important.*
*Bart: No.*
*Interviewer: You think it's okay that people can discriminate against you?*
*Bart: Yeah.*
*Hoysey: But I don't think it is, you've been in prison and served your sentence.*
*Bart: Say it's my fault for being in prison – no one else's. You've only got yourself to blame. (Hull)*

The Traveller tradition is of self-employment through extended family networks. Work includes farm labouring, fixing and selling scrap metal and making small items for sales at markets. But work is often about subsistence and 'doing what needs to be done' rather than conventional employment. In addition, many Traveller traditions, such as long periods of mourning in the event of bereavement, can make conventional work difficult to sustain.

The young Travellers identified a lack of work for travelling families, making their way of life economically unsustainable, as the main threat to their way of life.

> *There is no work for Travellers, no. Years ago they used to travel around the country doing different types of jobs around farms, but they are not needed any more. B (Belfast)*

The Traveller community traditionally has a different approach to the idea of work from settled people. As one explained:

> *From an early age we work, not to be paid but in order to survive and we see work as part of life and not something that you get paid for. We worked at the old jobs of recycling of materials and scrap metals. We did work around metal work and others had different skills like making things with their hands to sell to get food and clothes. The women were expected to take care of the home and it was not known for a girl to work outside the camp until she was married and had her own family. Then she was expected to do whatever she could to care for them, even if it meant begging for food. (Belfast)*

This notion of work as subsistence is fading, largely because the traditional types of work are increasingly hard to find. Most of the young people felt that change was inevitable, but felt cultural pressures which made it hard for them to adapt to conventional notions of work.

> *Work for us is different. It is very strange for us to be paid for work. Or the idea of working at set hours. This is hard to do. We always worked when we had to and in the time that suited us. Now you are expected to turn up at a certain time and work whether you are ready or not and that is hard for us to do. If we feel that something is more*

*important, like a wedding or a funeral or a sick relative, then we are inclined to do that and leave the work there. It is not so important to us. Family is everything and they come first.* **(Belfast)**

They also feared they would suffer discrimination when they applied for conventional jobs.

*Who would want to employ us? People would rather drive us out than give us a job and there is a terrible lot of hatred of the Travellers, about who they are and the way they live…. Even if we do get work it is only low-paid stuff and we are never trusted. People think we are all thieves.* **(Belfast)**

## The changing world of work

Most Real Deal participants recognised that the world of work had changed since their parents' generation. In some cases this meant the loss of previously secure jobs. For others it was simply the availability of jobs and the ability to move straightforwardly from one to another. For some, the world of security in which their parents had worked was almost impossible to imagine.

*Yeah, it used to be much more "You'll definitely have a job for life and a house for life" and it's a lot different from that now. You might get a job now but in a week you might be living in a box in the street again.*

*Stuff like a pension plan, you don't really hear of that any more. My mum and dad have are like "Oh, my pension plan", but what jobs have pension plans these days?* **(Edinburgh)**

Almost all recognised that academic qualifications were even more important than in previous generations. Some argued that 'softer' skills were as important in obtaining employment.

*I don't think education is really important, I don't think you need to be well educated to do a job. I've got no GCSEs but I reckon I could do a job just as well as someone with A levels. Life skills are more important, common sense.* **John (Durham)**

***Hoysey:*** *Being motivated, that will help you. Wanting to get a job.*
***P:*** *What's that thing – a good sense of humour.*
***Dunny:*** *Yeah, I think a good sense of humour because if you're a sad twat you're not going to get nowhere in life.* **(Hull)**

The decline of large-scale manufacturing has also seen a corresponding decline in trade union membership. Very few young people mentioned unions as an aspect of the world of work, but those who did were sceptical of their value.

***T:*** *The membership of unions is middle-aged. It's nae like for young folk.*

*D: But each time you've had to argue for your wages or your conditions, you're doing it on your own.*
*R: I can't see any union do anything to help for any young person. They're there for the majority of middle-aged workers. (Aberdeenshire)*

Very few of the young people suggested that women, even mothers with young children, should not be encouraged to work if they wanted to. With a few exceptions (the army, mining), they also felt that women should be able to do any job on an equal basis with men, though they recognised that this was not always the case in reality.

*In our society men are worried that women are going to have kids and then go and leave their job, it holds them back from getting better at their jobs.* **Jen**

*Women are better at some jobs than men and men are better at some jobs than women.* **Chunk**

*It should just be equal opportunities and that's an end to it, if a woman wants to work she should be able to.* **Smithy**

*It's about stereotypes though – in society, nurses are seen as female when they are clearly not always. It's just when you think of a nurse you think of a blue dress and a white hat.* **Marzy (all Durham)**

Mothers with young children, some participants felt, would be more likely to work if childcare were available.

*Yes, they should cos otherwise they could get too used to being at home all the time. And workplace crèches are more common now.* **Tanya**

*If a woman works it's for a healthy mind for herself and her child, cos she needs time out from that child.* **Christine**

*If there were better childcare, crèches and that, then more women might want to work.* **Lisa (all Durham)**

*I'd like to get out and have something worthwhile to get up for rather than just Richard and Judy. I would work if there was childcare. (Edinburgh)*

Others were unconvinced and unhappy about any suggestion of coercion.

*Mum said in America that they make single parents work after their children are ten months old. This woman said she had to put her kids in childcare, she had to turn up for a job and she said they were just making work for them. She said she wanted to look after her children and because if the kids were ill and they were late, they lost their job and they were on less benefit. They had to work and that is what Labour is thinking of doing in this country. They can't make me put my daughter to some stranger, pay someone else to look after her while I go and do something which didn't need done in the first place.* **E (Aberdeenshire)**

Even for those without children, the idea of the government encouraging people off benefits and into work was contentious. This was particularly the case where people felt that such policies were merely 'make work' schemes.

*You can't make jobs that are basically not there. They're just paying people to employ people until they don't get paid to employ them any more, if you see what I mean. It's a stupid idea.* **E (Aberdeenshire)**

## Pay and the minimum wage

A crop of current government initiatives such as the New Deal, implementation of the Social Chapter and the Working Families Tax Credit are aimed at reducing dependence and benefits and increasing the uptake of work, especially among the socially excluded. Many employment policies aim to help people get into work rather than improve the quality of work that people do.

The major reform aimed at improving working conditions, the national minimum wage, won widespread support among these young people, though many resented being excluded from it or on its lower rate because of age. Overall, low pay was one of the major sources of complaint,

*You don't get good pay though, do you? Young people don't get paid well. Getting paid £30 a week to work nine to five on a YT is a bit below the belt.* **Smithy (Durham)**

*H: My mum keeps on at me, when are your wages going up? I don't like to say when are you going to pay me some more? I did ask eventually and my wages did go up after a couple of months. But my mum said one of her cousins had just got a job at William Lows and he was getting £4 an hour.*
*U: I've had a lot of training to do what I do but the wages are still bad. It's a joke.*
*H: At my first job I was opening up. I had keys for the place and I was there one Saturday morning all by myself for four hours. I was only seventeen and paid £2.75 an hour but yet you have got all this responsibility. I was the only person in the whole building, the front of the building, the back of the building to do and all the jobs on the table to be done.* **(Aberdeenshire)**

*Some companies take advantage of your age. Like canvassing companies and fish companies, the hours that you do, you don't really get paid for, like canvassing, some places give you a bare wage … In fish filleting places, the hours you work, you don't get paid the right sort of money.* **Hoysey (Hull)**

*Why is there this discrimination? Why if you sixteen do you get paid less? I can't under-
stand it if you go into the same job as an eighteen year old or a 21 year old you get less
money.* **U** *(Aberdeenshire)*

*I can't believe that the minimum wage is not until you're 21. There is one from eighteen
to 21 but that's something ridiculously low. And if you're under eighteen, you can get
paid anything they like. In the [processing plant], you don't get paid £2 an hour until
you turn eighteen. A lot of people have to work there, the only place you can get a job is
in the factories or in the [processing plant].* **(Edinburgh)**

Others felt they were not given enough information about minimum wage or other employee
rights, including the Working Hours Directive.

*X: I went on an employment legislation workshop – there's all this stuff I didn't realise.
Even the fact that Saturday workers are entitled to two weeks' holiday pro rata, which I
don't think any Saturday or part-time worker knows.
Y: It's not the sort of thing they are going to tell you.
X: This came in October 1st. Did anyone notice anything in the paper about this? You're
also not supposed to work for more than 48 hours a week for a six-week period.*
**(Edinburgh)**

In general the level of the minimum wage was less controversial, though many thought it should
be slightly higher,

*I think there should be some kind of worthwhile minimum hourly wage – £3.60 is too
low I think especially for over 25. It's very difficult to survive on that – you're going
home with a very small pay packet. I said I'd be willing to work for £3 an hour, but
that's because I don't have many skills and if I was doing some really menial task, then
I'd be willing to do it because I don't have anyone to support except myself and basically
that's like babysitting or something for £3 an hour. A minimum wage for people to survive, you definitely need at least £4 or £5 an hour otherwise they are having to work
themselves into the ground in a job they are not enjoying just to make ends meet.* **Tigger**
**(Oxford)**

## New Deal

The New Deal for the young unemployed was introduced during the course of the consultation and
only a few participants had any real experience of it. Its compulsory element was of concern to
some, while others were annoyed that they had to wait six months before being eligible.

Some questioned whether the policy can work during a period of recession when most employers
are firing people. There were also concerns that the New Deal will push some people into working
in the illegal economy or into crime because they do not want to take any of the options.

Those young people who had experienced New Deal had varied opinions of it.

> *I sat down at a desk and he looked on the computer at what my interests were, motor mechanics and sport and recreation. He was being friendly and he talked to us for an hour, talking about what would happen and he said that in five years he would like to see us and I'd thank him for getting us a job.* **Big Dunc (Durham)**

For some, it had been a positive experience.

> *I've been six months unemployed and I went to the dole and wanted to go to college and the dole are going to pay for me to do an HND at college on computer support, which is pretty good, cos I still get all my benefits and my housing and my Giro.*

> *I've had quite a good experience of New Deal. I'm doing a course at college in dance music, which is the biggest blag I've ever heard of. Go to college late, sit in front of a keyboard and a big workstation and just start writing music all day and the government is paying for me to do that, which is good.* **(Edinburgh)**

Others felt that the system of 'personal advisers' was not working as well as it might and was not as integrated into existing schemes as it could be.

> *When I went in and signed on, it [the New Deal] was if I didn't have a choice. The lady basically asked me what type of work I was looking for, even though they should know by now. So I said to her retail and she goes to me, "Here you are going to be put on the New Deal. You have to queue up to see the adviser." I was like on a course and I told them from day one and filled out a new form as they didn't know anything.* **Ahmed (Camberwell)**

There was also concern that the New Deal would mean the end of study not listed under New Deal options.

> *I really do want to do this course. That's why I took it in the first place to give me a better chance to get into the stage of retail that I want to do, which is the management stage of it … And now they have basically bunged the New Deal thing in front of me this morning and told me if they find a job for me in retail, I have to drop the course, and I don't want to.* **Ahmed (Camberwell)**

Some of those who have not yet experienced the New Deal were sceptical, expecting a re-run of previous training schemes. Many of the young people had experienced such schemes before and felt they had been exploited, not given any training and not had the chance to learn useful skills. One young man in Hull contrasted them with what he regarded as 'proper' apprenticeships.

> *It's on the job training, isn't it? Work placements and apprenticeships are two different things. On apprenticeships – you get paid quite a lot of money and you're learning like*

*all the skills and in a work placement you get like £40 a week and you don't learn all the skills like what you would do if you were on an apprenticeship.* **Hoysey (Hull)**

Even with the promises of the New Deal, many were concerned about having to do something they were not interested in for low wages.

*I think if they are going to do that then they should have a wider range of options that would fit for everybody.* **Lisa (Durham)**

In other cases there was a disagreement about the merits of the system.

*Dunny: New Deal is totally different.*
*Hoysey: Bart, New Deal, they've got better things and you choose where you want to go.*
*Bart: Yeah, and if you don't like none of the stuff they've got, then they say fair enough then, you don't want to go on New Deal, and you're saying that you don't want to work at all and they stop your money.*
*Hoysey: But if you're unemployed then you must be wanting to find a job. If you've been unemployed for six months you'd take anything going to get a job.*
*Interviewer: So you think it is fair?*
*Bart: So you'd take a job where the boss is a right arsehole, telling you to make cups of tea all the time?*
*Hoysey: But Bart, I know for a fact that they've got stuff to do with cars and mechanics.*
*Interviewer: Do you think young people will be interested in New Deal because it means £10 more?*
*Hoysey: Yeah.*
*Dunny: All I can say is the New Deal is classed as a six-month trial first, if you get a full-time job afterwards then you get it, it's about helping people get a job.*
*Interviewer: So you think it's a genuine attempt to get people into work?*
*Dunny: Yeah, it is.* **(Hull)**

The concern identified above about 'make work' schemes also applied to New Deal. Some worried that the jobs were not real and could not be sustainable.

*They are trying to make jobs where there aren't any, so how can the companies keep them on when they didn't need that extra person in the first place?*
**E (Aberdeenshire)**

For the Traveller community, the notion of New Deal and other government training schemes was hard to adapt to, though some recognised that 'we have to change our attitudes to lots if things, if we are to survive'. None had as yet experienced New Deal, but some had done other government training schemes and found them wanting.

*We should be getting training in the kind of work that we want to do and we should be getting help with the skills that we already possess. We are very good with our hands and if there were more training at our level, it would be great. Some of the language that is used goes way over our heads and it is hard to understand what it is all about. No one ever asks us what we want to be trained in and when we do ask for what we want, it is never possible to get funding and so on. What we would really like is to have training that is not so complicated and is really suited to our needs. The problem is we have so many needs, it is hard to know where to get started.* **(Belfast)**

## One to one findings

Most of the young people interviewed one to one wanted to work. They wanted to 'stimulate their brains', they wanted to be 'useful to people' and interact with people, but most of all they wanted to earn money so they could be independent. To be earning was, for some, extremely important to their self-respect.

*I would sooner work for my living. I would rather die than not work for my living and be given freebies. This is the reason why I don't like being on a Giro. This is the reason why although I am on a Giro I still go out busking because I don't like having all my money for free because I still consider that being free, you know. Yes I'm looking for work. Yes I'm doing this. Yes I'm doing that. But at the end of the day I'm still getting money for doing absolutely nothing, and for me I can't feel comfy with that. You know, for me it's like abnormal. They're giving me money: why?* **Marcus, White, 20, London**

*Well, at one point work meant everything. If I wasn't working or sleeping or eating, that was it. I did a full-time day job and did bar work at night, and it was killing me, but I did it just to support my girlfriend and son because she didn't bring any money into the house. Work's good. Work makes you feel better. I don't feel as good as I do now, only when I'm working. It makes me feel a happier person. More in control of my life. I don't have to depend on this little piece of paper which comes through the post with £60 on it and "Here you are, here's two week's money." Christ, I could be earning £160 in one week and that's more like it.* **Adrian, White British, 22, Devon**

Earning money was also fundamentally important.

**Interviewer:** *And how important is work to you?*
*Important enough to stay alive, you need work to get money to stay alive, to support yourself and your family if you've got one. Keeps you off the streets and stop being bored.* **Paul, White, 19, London**

*Especially being in a position where, eventually, you're hoping to get your own place and you need money to put down. So, that is top of my list – work. It has to be work.* **Nick, London**

Work was also seen as being an important form of activity in its own right, to stop people from becoming 'bored' and to give their lives a structure. Some explained that working helped them through life, keeping them off alcohol or drugs. Another commented that his home town had a problem with young people selling drugs because there were no jobs available and dealing was one way of making money.

> *Interviewer: How important is work to you?*
> *Extremely important because I get so bored. If I am walking around all day I get so bored and then I start thinking what job shall I do now? Who shall I rip off? You know what I mean? I get so bored, so many things happening in my head. Just get myself straight and get back straight back into work, don't care where as long as I have a bit of grain coming in.* **Les**

> *Interviewer: So work is the source of income, what else does work mean to you other than earning income?*
> *Something to do. Just stop me drinking, I used to have a good job, you have enough money to buy yourself a house, but you know drink.* **Simon, Black British, 21, London**

> *For me work's just been the safety net, as I said, so I don't fall into the pit-holes as some of my outside friends have done and turned to crime, drugs, supporting bad habits, having children just to get accommodation or just becoming a statistic because they depend on income support and so on and so forth.* **Suzanne, Afro-Caribbean, 20, London**

Although most wanted to work, there were extreme difficulties in finding a job. An initial problem was that of the 'homelessness cycle'. Once a person became homeless, some explained, they had no fixed address and without a fixed address employers would not take them on. As in the group discussions, some felt that employers were also hostile to people who gave hostel addresses. Another concern was that being homeless meant that they were out of work and that having gaps in a CV was frowned upon by employers. Others pointed out that having a criminal record made it difficult for them to find work.

> *I want to work. I've been wanting to work all my life … If you want a job from them, you've got to have a place to stay. If you want a place to stay, you've got to have a job.* **Gavin, European, 24, Devon**

> *It's important but at the end of the day it's hard when you've a criminal record to get a job and plus like in the hostel you've never really settled in in a hostel, it's like you've got to end up leaving and changing addresses and things like that so you ain't got no permanent address. It's hard to get a job that way and all, and like when you've been homeless for a while it's hard to get a job anyway because they're going to ask what you've been doing in the last couple of years and when you say, "Oh well nothing", it don't look very good on a CV, does it? So it's hard.*

> *My criminal record. That's what really ruins me for work. My criminal record is, well, how can I explain, it's about seven sheets … Really at the end of the day, I know the criminal record puts them off, but at the end of the day, they shouldn't go by that. They should*

*go by the person themselves. Instead of saying, "We don't want him here because of like what he's done in the past." The way I think is, what is in the past is the past. How are people meant to get a job if you ain't going to give them a trial? If you can't like give 'em a test, and see how they work out and that?* **John, White British, 25, London**

Another barrier was a lack of experience, with some arguing that because they lacked experience employers were unwilling to take give them a job. As one explained, 'You can't normally get a job unless you're given a chance.'

As in the consultation groups, the level of wages was also perceived as a barrier. Those in London compared the wages available with the money required to rent accommodation. On average, they explained rental was about £70 to £80 a week and as the available jobs paid around £4 an hour, it was not worth their working. Others commented on some hostel regulations, explaining that the steep rise in prices for those working compared with those not working was a major disincentive to work. Some, those particularly aggrieved by the low wages available, admired drug dealers as they were able to make large amounts of money quickly.

*For me personally it's not enough to work for £4 an hour, after tax and by the time, hostels are very expensive, this place if I work I have to pay altogether £172 so I can't work until I live in a place like long term which may be about 80 odd pounds a week.* **May, English-Irish, 23, London**

*But it's [bar work and catering] not very well paid. Most of them are lucky to take home £150 a week. But if you've got a flat and you're paying £70 a week – or even a room at that price. The incentive should be with the Housing Benefit … I've looked into it and they say there is that support, but the way they work it out is you get £5 more than what you would have got on the Giro. I'm sorry, but I don't think anyone is really willing to work 40 hours a week just for the sake of getting an extra £5 in their pocket.* **David, White British, 24, London**

Training schemes were also criticised for the low payments.

*They can put you on a crappy sort of £45-a-week Youth Training Scheme and by the end of it you've learned absolutely nothing. You're just skint all the time. I've done it before.* **Tim, White British, 17, Devon**

# Conclusions

Both the group consultation and the individual interviews produced strong conclusions about learning and working which are directly relevant to future policy.

■ Most of these young people's experience of education is negative. They feel that school does not provide the skills and knowledge that they really need, and that provision is often too rigid and inappropriately delivered.

■ Many recognised the pressures that teachers and schools face. However, they also feel strongly that more could be done to make school more stimulating, relevant and accessible.

■ The curriculum should be broader and include a much stronger emphasis on the practical skills and understanding needed to face the immediate challenges of young adulthood.

■ Teachers should be better trained in how to relate to young people rather than simply in the subjects they teach. Many of the young people felt that teachers were not really committed to them and that they were discriminated against in favour of those more likely to succeed in exams.

■ Counselling and guidance services are largely inadequate and could make a huge difference to young people's capacity to participate productively in education.

■ Schools often fail to recognise the impact that disruption and trauma in young people's personal lives can have on their ability to participate in school.

■ Most saw bullying and peer pressure as major barriers to educational achievement in school.

■ Some felt that the school curriculum between fourteen and sixteen was particularly irrelevant.

■ Most of the young people recognised the importance of education for later achievement, especially work. Those who had left education before sixteen were less likely to see it in any positive way.

■ Those with experience of college and post-compulsory education were more likely to be positive about education and to praise the different atmosphere and structure of colleges in comparison to schools.

■ Involving young people, particularly those with experience similar to the risks facing others, was suggested by many and strongly endorsed by most. Peer education schemes were praised.

■ Many felt that they were inadequately prepared for the choices and challenges they faced when they left school.

■ Lifelong learning was an idea that few recognised.

■ Participation in higher education was seen as difficult and inaccessible. Many had strong concerns about lack of financial support and said that higher education was becoming available only to those with strong family support.

■ Several of the young homeless people interviewed one to one had been forced by circumstance to leave higher or further education and felt stuck in a gap between their relatively high qualifications and lack of employment experience.

■ These young people's experience of work was varied but largely negative.

■ There was strong recognition that the world of work had changed dramatically but little confidence about coping with the new challenges.

■ Many had experienced exploitation and unfairness of work.

■ Most people's experience was in low-skill, casualised employment. Most said that pressure, working conditions and insecurity made it very difficult to sustain work in the jobs that they could get. Few had worked at the same job for a long period of time.

■ Most felt that careers advice and guidance had been of little help, and that information about opportunities, entitlements and available support was largely inadequate.

■ Almost all had experience of the informal economy and some of criminal work such as handling drugs. Some felt that barriers such as criminal records prevented them from any chance of finding work. Others said that the money they could earn from such work made it difficult to accept legal employment.

■ Low pay was identified by almost all as a major barrier to long-term participation in work. Many felt that the benefits system made it even more difficult. Many praised the minimum wage, but were angry at the exclusion of younger people.

■ Most were committed to the idea of equal opportunities in employment. There were few strong views about what kinds of work women and men should do.

■ The New Deal received mixed reviews. Many young people saw it as worthwhile and different from past programmes. Others were sceptical and distrustful of the government's motives. Most of the older Real Deal participants had negative experience of training schemes. Many were also sceptical of the idea that governments could make jobs that did not really exist.

■ There was a clear and wide gap between experiences of education and the kinds of work experience which the young people had gained. Although many said that qualifications were needed to get work, few had positive experience of education and work opportunities fitting together in a coherent way.

■ Parents and family were less influential in making work decisions than in education.

# What we need

## Services and support

Discussions of the subjects in earlier chapters raised several important findings about the kinds of services and support the young people in Real Deal groups felt that they needed. These are largely covered in discussion of specific areas. Some of the most important common threads are:

- The importance and influence of family support
- The need for services which are effective before things reach crisis point
- The need for better guidance and counselling
- The need for services to recognise and respond to individual differences between young people
- The need to be listened to and respected
- The need for services and facilities which are available and accessible to people between the ages of fourteen and nineteen.

### One to one findings

This chapter presents material on public services and other forms of support from the individual interviews with homeless young people. They have had experience of a wide range of services, both before and during homelessness. Many had past experiences of social services or had been in care. Others, generally more recently, had experience of job centres, the police, housing services and Citizens Advice Bureaux. Most attitudes towards government services were negative. Few felt that the services had actively had failed them: the thinking was more that the help or support they would have liked was simply not there. Some expressed hostility and fear towards particular services, most notably the police and social services.

One of the most striking themes was the criticism that people within specific organisations had failed to understand their problem or listen to their viewpoint. In one account, a girl described how, having been noticeably beaten by her father, her school brought together Social Services, her teachers, medical staff, the police and her parents. She did not attend the meeting because she did not want to see her parents. In her absence, the meeting decided that what had occurred was just a domestic argument. As the girl explained this 'cut me up badly' (emotionally) as her father had 'actually kicked the bathroom door in so he'd get at me.' Another who felt no one had helped him commented:

*Well, they [Social Services] really didn't do anything for me, just put me in a [home] and just left me there, every time I went to go and see them they weren't there, my social worker wasn't there.* **Paul, White, 19, London**

*Well, Social Services, if they'd listened to me in the first place, maybe I wouldn't be in the position I'm in now. So that would have saved a hell of a lot of hassle.* **Nick, London**

The second criticism was that rules and regulations were too rigid. Since becoming homeless, a high proportion had experienced difficulties in getting help, particularly in terms of benefits and accommodation. Lack of identification had proved problematic for some as they had been unable to register with housing and employment services. Age and eligibility was felt to be a problem for young people aged between sixteen and eighteen, both in terms of the housing and unemployment benefits available and access to support. As a seventeen year old explained:

*They [Social Services] said they can't deal with me because I'm seventeen and they only deal with under sixteens, so I went to the housing place and they said they couldn't help me again because I wasn't priority and I burst into tears.* **Janette, Afro-Caribbean, 18, London**

*They [the Council] reckon I'm not a priority need to be moved, because as far as they're concerned my mum has got a three-bedroom flat and she had no right to kick me out. I should go to Social Services, but then Social Services can't do nothing for me, because I'm not under sixteen, or sixteen. I'm seventeen. And the Council can't do nothing until I'm eighteen. So I'm stuck in the middle.* **Beth, 17, London**

Others raised the definitions of homelessness and priority homelessness. As one person despairing of the distinction put it, 'everybody is a priority case if they're homeless'. Another felt a result of this was that 'some girls might get pregnant in order to get a flat'.

*Homelessness ... Not everybody can help losing accommodation previously. It's not always in their power to keep hold of accommodation they've got, and they should not be classed as "continuously homeless" or just, you know, because somebody thinks, without even hearing the person out. I mean, for example like, you've got a job to go to, you've got a choice of your job or your accommodation. And you want the job more than the accommodation, then you'll go for the job. Then something can happen and you can lose your house. But if you lose a house, because of the job, you get cast as "intentionally homeless", so you never get re-housed for the next five years.* **Gavin, European, 24, Devon**

Another difficulty was highlighted by younger people who had been offered accommodation. They felt unable to accept the housing because the location was dangerous or run-down, and because of the prospect of having no support. Some of those who had accepted such accommodation had left it, lived with friends and then become homeless.

*Yes, but all I kept getting offered was you can either go back or we'll put you in a B&B or we'll put you into a flat and I wasn't ready to be in a flat by myself and the area that I was offered I knew that I couldn't live there anyway whether I wanted to or not, I just couldn't. It was on a big estate and I just worried about being harassed and things like that. Those were all the problems they had at the time, so I couldn't really say, "No, I don't want it."* **Magenta, Black British, 22, London**

The police faired worst in the young people's views. Many voiced general hostility and others argued that the police were unsympathetic to homeless people, treating them as 'animals'. The sense that the police 'hassled' rather than helped was widespread.

*I'm very anti-police, especially the way they treat the homeless, they've got their special squad set up for us, they do nothing but hassle us, our case 24/7, so they're supposed to be set up to help us.* **Cara, British, 22, London**

Another frequent comment was that young people were often unaware of what help was available: they did not know the 'system'. Many pointed out the difficulties they faced when they became homeless without knowing what to do about it or who to speak to. This prompted some to suggest that schools, in addition to teaching young people about 'drugs and stuff, they should tell people about homelessness and what to do if you find yourself without somewhere to live'. Another person suggested that signing on and getting government help was alien to her and that she would have benefited from advice on what was available.

*The services what they've got, they can help, but they're not publicised in any shape or form for young people to know that. If they get into this situation they can't turn round and say, "Well, I know where I can go to get some help." It's really like you have to dig and delve rather than just knowing instantly that certain things that you know instantly, like Childline for instance.* **Jim, 20, London**

*I think, I mean just getting in, I've managed to get into the system. I think there's a lot of help to be done in just getting people into it. I mean, I've spent a couple of years completely outside it all, didn't exist as far as anybody was concerned. And I mean, now I'm on the road to getting where I want to go. And once you get into services and you find out and connect to one thing you can connect to everything, but if you never connect to the first part then you never ever reach any of that.* **Ruby, White European, 20, London**

### Suggestions for improvement

Given that many felt 'lost' when they initially needed help, it is not surprising that information about available services was a high priority.

*I think they should inform us more of our rights, what we are allowed to have and not have sort of things, because it's all a blur to me let alone anybody else. I think there should both be more information instead of having to go there and sit down and, "What about this? What about this? What about this?"* **Adrian, White British, 22, Devon**

*They should put it [information about available support] on TVs. They should put it on radios – the radio stations that teenagers most listen to. They should put them up in schools and colleges, billboards and let it be known.* **Dana, Black, 18, London**

Suggestions for improving services centred around personalisation. Many young people felt that someone sitting down, talking to them about their situation and relating this to what was available would have been beneficial. One idea was that younger people were more able to relate to young people experiencing difficulties and should be more involved in service provision. For the same reason, it was felt that employing people with life experiences similar to the people using the services would be useful. Some called for specialists who would help them through the system.

Taking an individual approach was considered essential by many. Some suggested that benefits should also be worked out on an individual basis so they suited people's exact needs. In particular young people did not like being 'swapped around' between advisers. Some, who had experienced the New Deal were positive, particularly about having one adviser who talked to them about their situation and provided more long-term support. The ideal of a claimant adviser as counsellor came through in a number of interviews.

*Other people could come in with their problems, there would be a different section for each thing, or they could see an open adviser who they could go to and say, "Look, I've had this happen at work, what can I do? What do you see the best situation is?" And at some times it's not even a situation, it's just that they feel down, they're not in a right frame of mind, and a counsellor could help that.* **Janette, Afro-Caribbean, 18, London**

Many also felt that they had been pushed between different departments before finally getting to the right person or before a particular problem was sorted out.

*I think the benefits and the housing benefit and the social should be a lot more linked, because they don't know what each other are doing. I signed on a couple of weeks ago and I wanted to get my money on the same day so I could buy a cooker that was being sold, which is fair enough, I'd signed on to get paid on that day but the job centre where I sign on said, "We haven't got the authority to give out Giros any more, you've got to wait until it's sent out." They said, "You'll have to go down to the DSS." I went down to the DSS and waited for two hours and they said, "It's nothing to do with us, it's down to the job centre, if they want to give it to you they can give it to you."* **Anthony, White British, 21, London**

A few felt that some forms of support might stop people from addressing their situation as actively as they needed to.

*That [being given more benefits] wouldn't stop me but it would stop a lot of people. It's easy to get bogged down if you're in a comfortable position where you really don't have to do anything. It's easy to get stuck doing nothing at all.* **Anthony, White British, 21, London**

## Homeless services

The young people interviewed individually had used a variety of services. These included Shelter, New Horizons, London Connnection, Barnado's, St Vincent's and Centrepoint. Such services were generally felt to be helpful, especially those which took a personal interest.

*The London Connection is totally different because everybody is really asking how you are; asking how your problems are; is there anything wrong? How's it going, how's looking for a place going? It builds up your confidence because it's like someone taking an interest in what you're actually doing and how you're doing it. Well, they're giving you advice on how to do it and how to approach it in the right manner.* **Jim, 20, London**

There were also some specific criticisms. One was the curfew rules placed on some hostels. This applied to rules during the day stipulating when residents had to be out of the hostel and the rules stating what time in the evening they had to be in by. Both were felt to be restrictions on individual freedom. Some also commented that, when hostels did not let people in during the day, they found themselves with nothing to do. Some felt they needed someone to talk to during the day. Others pointed out that not having anything to do could cause crime. Day centres and hostels which ran day trips or organised daytime activities were praised.

*They should put on more recreational stuff. You know, not just sport and that, but sort of entertainment stuff. Sort of youth clubs or something ... I mean, most of the kids on the street, they are like, "Oh, we're really bored and got nothing to do." That's when all the thefts happen and it's bad apples, isn't it?* **Tim, White British, 17, Devon**

*I'd make it so you have access to be inside somewhere every day. You know, you leave the hostel at 8 o'clock in the morning, have somewhere you can go at 8 o'clock in the morning, and then you could kick about there until it's time to come back in and go to bed.* **Bill, Scottish, 20, London**

The relationship with the hostel worker was felt to be very important, with many confiding in a particular worker as their main source of support. Some concern was, however, voiced about confidentiality. As one young woman explained, some hostel workers tend to work in different hostels and this had caused her difficulties in that she felt they knew too much about her.

*I wish workers didn't move from place to place because I mean I know I got a shock when I was in here and when I realised that I'd seen Linda in Ronald Place and I really thought, oh, maybe I should just leave now, but I didn't and you know I've since bumped into her, is it Mark from Ronald Place, at Fresh Start and it's like, oh my god, I can't get*

*away from these people, you know, if I want to sort of re-do myself, I'm going to be total-
ly sorted now, and there's always somebody who says, "Ah, I know the dirt on you."*
**Ruby, White European, 20, London**

## Forms of support

The young people involved in one to one interviews, just like those in the group consultation, also
had clear views about the kinds of support that they needed in order to survive and to make
progress.. Suggestions that guidance, advice or 'having someone to talk to' has helped or would help
came through in discussion of all aspects of life. Most felt that they lacked effective support. The
two main forms of support were emotional and practical. Emotional support was felt important to
build up people's self-esteem and confidence. People talked both about not being able to turn to
their family and being unable to confide in people outside the home because no such support existed. Being homeless was felt to compound these problems.

> *Well, I don't really get support. I had to learn from quite young to be able to deal with
> things like that. No it's … It can be quite lonely sometimes, but being independent so
> long I'm used to it.* **Paul, Irish-English, 24, London**

> *The only people I support, I got my family and that but I don't really like my family,
> don't really get involved with them, but I suppose they're there in a way, do you know
> what I mean?* **Cara, British, 22, London**

> *Help I need? I need a lot of support. I need a lot of guidance. Sometimes I might just
> need a little a shoulder to cry on sometimes, know what I mean, and they say that men
> don't cry but that's a load of rubbish to be quite honest.* **Callum, White, 24, London**

> *Well, I mainly need support from here [the hostel] and friends, people around me, the
> media to have a good portrayal of a social worker (my ambition is to be a social worker).
> I need job experience, and having a good education, that's the main thing.* **Janette,
> Afro-Caribbean, 18, London**

Associated with the lack of support networks was a strong sense that many homeless young people
were unwilling and unable to trust others. As one person replied when asked who she trusted,
'Nobody. If I was to be completely honest, I don't trust anybody. I trust myself.' These young people were extremely cautious when it came to trusting, preferring to rely on themselves rather than
risk being hurt or having their trust abused. Some found the subject of trust, support and relations
distressing and asked to change the subject.

> *Yes, never trusted anyone. Some people say it's a bad thing and it's really sad to go
> through life without really trusting anyone. But if you don't trust someone they can't let
> you down really, can they?* **Magenta, Black British, 22, London**

*Survival tactics, I adapt, yeah, if I can't adapt I curl up in a ball. I would basically describe my tactics as a hedgehog. Yeah, you see because I put up spikes. No one can get too close to me to hurt me, metaphoric spikes so no one can get too close, I won't let anybody in.* **Marcus, White, 20, London**

*I think I'm proud about how I've coped with the independence and living – not under mother and father's wing.* **Jim, 20, London**

*I don't like to get close to people so there isn't anyone I could. Because I keep people distant, then no one can hurt me and at the same time if I am in trouble I can't really ask them.* **Tim, Black, 24, London**

Self-reliance was mentioned often in the interviews, and many were proud to be able to work through their own troubles and look after themselves. For many the lack of support had made them very independent. When asked who they went to for help a common response was 'myself'. However, people often also said that this reflected their circumstances rather than being and ideal choice.

*With me, as I said I'm one of these people that are very, very rational thinkers and when I get in a problem it seems to bring out the best in a sense and I can scrape myself out, I've found that it's one of my strong points.* **Marcus, White, 20, London**

One person felt that a lack of financial support could result in people getting into crime or 'bad habits'.

*In terms of education if you're living on your own and you decide you want to further your education and go to university you get your housing benefits taken away and so on, I just don't think it's very encouraging and then you do get young people doing alternatives such as getting pregnant, crime, drugs, robberies, just to support either an education or a bad habit which they might have so I don't generally think that we get a lot of support at all.* **Suzanne, Afro-Caribbean, 20, London**

Sources of support included friends, family, religious beliefs, homelessness agencies and, for some, certain workers whom they relied and confided in. However there were caveats. Most spoke about just one close friend or one homelessness worker whom they would confide in, with some explaining that relying on people could cause problems if they were unable to help. It was also suggested by some that friends may not be the best people to help. As one person who had alcohol problems explained, 'They're only going to say, "Don't worry about it, mate. Have another drink."' Others felt friends had problems of their own and that it was too much to ask them to deal with 'other people's problems'.

Some felt that too much support could make people dependent.

**Interviewer:** *Who do you count on for support?*

*Organisations, Centrepoint, Barnardo's, if I do find it a lot more stressful than I can handle then I may go to family but I tend to try and work things out on my own really, just be, I've moved out so I tend to try and do things by myself so that I can feel that I've made an achievement and done a lot more on my own as a young person.* **Suzanne, Afro-Caribbean, 20, London**

*I think you can help people too much, if you see what I mean. I think if you start helping people too much, they get reliant on that too much and they don't do nothing for themselves, which is not a good thing.* **David, White British, 24, London**

Many talked about the kind of support they would like and what would have helped them when they were younger. There were two principal kinds of support: emotional and practical. For most, it was the emotional support that they felt would be most beneficial. As one person said, 'I think all the help I need is people telling me that I can do it. I mean, "You can do it."' The need for long-term support was also mentioned frequently and, for some who had close relations with particular homelessness workers, they felt they would like to maintain some level of contact even when they no longer lived in the hostel. The Centrepoint Peer Education scheme, in which homeless people mentor other homeless people was praised by some.

The need for support early in life was also a common theme. Some felt that support at school, for example, counselling, would have been valuable. Many also said that they needed support when they first left home or care. One idea for early support was an after-school club in which people could do activities, such as pottery, but could also talk to someone and get advice if they needed it. The suggestion was also made that young people need educating about homelessness.

*I think there should be a certain amount of time for caring before you leave home. Some are on their own. I think they should be given a set time to find out how to budget money and cook and all that sort of stuff and when they have done it all then they can move in somewhere.* **Tom, White Scottish, 24, London**

*Because I was not trained on how to be independent, I just used my house as a place to have parties and I was on my own. I never had any support whatsoever and I was skint. The government wouldn't give me any money to like decorate my flat and stuff, but I'm glad they never really, because I was not ready at that time, I was definitely not ready to have my own place. There should have been something in between that when I left care to when I moved in to help me adjust to what it was going to be like when I did eventually come to be on my own.* **Sharon, Scottish, 24, London**

*Well, especially emotional advice like, someone who tells you they can help you with your emotional stuff and whatever. You need someone to talk to when you first leave home, to have counselling or something.* **Lynda, African, 20, London**

# Conclusions

■ Many of these young people take strong pride in their self-reliance, and their trust has to be carefully won.

■ They value sustained, personal support and guidance and often rely on one particular figure for regular support.

■ Being listened to and respected as an individual was identified as the single biggest factor that would improve the provision of services.

■ Public services were criticised for inflexibility and for lack of information.

■ Emotional and practical support were identified as the two greatest needs, and many said that more effective help earlier in life could have prevented the situation that they now faced.

■ Many valued family support, but felt that they could not rely on it.

# What we think

## Politics and government

### Findings

Overall, the general sense of alienation and marginalisation which the consultation revealed is reflected in the young people's views of politics, politicians and government. This picture, however, is not straightforward. Some Real Deal participants were more positive about particular aspects of politics and about individual politicians. The young people in both the consultation groups and the one to one interviews offered clear ideas about what would encourage and support their active involvement in the political system. Trust, respect and communication were paramount, alongside the perception that it was only possible to take more interest in politics when the fundamentals of life – having homes, jobs and futures – were more secure.

Many began with a deep cynicism about politicians. Financial questions and scandals, in particular, seemed to affect people's views strongly, with many participants saying they felt politicians were about 'making money'. It is important to recognise that this overall view of politics and government did not extend to all forms of political participation or to all politicians. Many of the young people were motivated by and knowledgeable about forms of political engagement that do not fit into the formal systems of electoral politics and public consultation.

Although many had little formal knowledge of how systems of government functioned, they did have a strong sense of the issues that they cared about. The overwhelming impression was of a system which failed to engage with their experience or concerns and therefore did little to encourage or reward more active involvement. This criticism was directed mainly at politicians, but similar complaints are also voiced about education, work, police and other officials.

Politicians were also criticised for not doing what they are supposed to do, even though in some cases the young person had only the vaguest idea of what they expected.

> *I don't know, but they don't do nowt. What are they supposed to do? They don't make things better, like they're supposed to.* **Emily (Hull)**

The consultation provided some evidence that other forms of political engagement , such as environmentalism, or issues which directly touched people's lives, such as asylum and immigration, motivated some of the young people to engage more directly. As one young woman in the Edinburgh group explained:

> It's when you hear about something and you think, "This is going to fucking destroy my life". That's when you get provoked. Like the Criminal Justice and Public Order Bill, Travellers, the Poll Tax or whatever. When something like that happens you think, "How can I let this happen? I want to get up there with my big banner." **(Edinburgh)**

Many of the most marginalised, such as Travellers, those who had been in trouble with the law or those who were not attending school, were the most likely to feel disengaged from politics and to profess deep cynicism. One of the young male Travellers from the Belfast group explained:

> To tell you the truth, there is not much that we know about the government, or care either. I suppose they are the people who tell us to move on and they are also the people who pay us our dole and children's allowance. But to be honest there is not a lot that we know about the government. I couldn't name any of the ones here. We never had any business with them. It does not make a lot of difference to our lives one way or another and we don't see how the government would make any difference to us. We have been living like this for a long time and we have never got anything from the government, only hardship. **(Belfast)**

For some, the impact of material disadvantage and the social and cultural conditions accompanying it help to explain their sense of disconnection. Many felt that just getting by from day to day takes all of their energy. As two young people from London commented:

> Young people aren't interested in politics anyway. When they go down the job centre, they are concerned about signing on. They don't want to know about the system. **Gerald**

> At the end of the day, the reason why most of us don't vote is that we are homeless and unemployed. We are trying to get ourselves some money and a permanent place to live, a job. We are too busy doing other things that are more important in our lives than voting. I don't really care who runs the country, as long as things are made fair. **Ahmed (Camberwell)**

Many felt that the distinctions between the main parties were unclear and that the voting choices they faced did not reflect the structure of their concerns or preferences.

> It feels like it's difficult to choose between the main parties now, they all seem the same, as New Labour is almost Conservative you know. So yeah, you could vote for a change but they're not offering much change really. **Jen (Durham)**

## One to one findings

The views of young people interviewed individually mirrored those found in the groups. Most were cynical and disillusioned about politics and the political process. Very few had looked into voting and even fewer had voted. Politics was said to be 'irrelevant' and 'boring' and few claimed to have an interest in politics. Many felt that engaging in politics would not achieve anything. Politics was seen as something which had 'no bearing on [their] lives'. As people explained:

> *Because of the situation I am in now, most of these decisions they make and the changes they make on a day-to-day basis, have no bearing on my life. If you're a businessman, and you've got lots of money and investments and all that, then it probably does. It makes a very big difference, doesn't it? But to me, it doesn't really touch my life.* **David, White British, 24, London**

> *I've got no plans to vote on any elections or anything. I don't feel that it makes much difference. I haven't noticed any difference in my life in the change of government. The only change of government that's been when I've been alive, I've not noticed any difference. I don't think there would be any difference.* **Anthony, White British, 21, London**

The view that politicians care only 'about what is good for them and their kind of people' echoed throughout most interviews. Associated with this feeling of isolation was some people's view that their opinions do not count.

> *No. Not really. I'm just not a political person, I don't really care one way or the other. Although some people get really upset when you say that, they think, "Oh you should care, it's your world, your country too", but you know, I never think what I think is going to make any difference at the end of the day, I'd rather use my energies thinking about something else that matters for me.* **Magenta, Black British, 22, London**

> *No [I don't vote]. I don't think it's going to make any difference a young homeless irrelevant person like me, I'm not going to make any difference.* **Sharon, Scottish, 24, London**

Attitudes towards politicians were equally bleak, with politicians viewed as crooks who take back handers, media-driven fakes, out to get power and generally uninterested in ordinary people's lives. Political spin appeared not to have much currency with these young people, and they were hostile towards being told about initiatives without having felt any tangible effect themselves.

> *I mean you've got Tony Blair with a big cheesy grin on his face, you know what I mean, all the time. He's just doing that, it's just a ploy thing, it's just a publicity thing to make him look good, you know what I mean, but then they said New Labour and New Britain and all this, that's a load of rubbish, useless, it's just the same as when Margaret Thatcher was in power.* **Michael, Irish, 20, London**

As in the groups, the view was expressed that political parties were no different from each other. As politicians *per se* Labour and the Conservatives were treated the same: 'You know they'll say they'll do things and they don't do them.'

> *They all speak exactly the same, they always tell something and they wonder what you say, don't listen to what they say, they all mumble, they say one thing and do the other.*
> **Michael, Irish, 20, London**

The perception that Labour and Conservative Party policy are similar was widespread and for those who held it this was another disincentive to vote. As one person put it:

> *Labour used to be more about the people, but now they're just like the Tory government were really, so there's no point in voting, and the other parties, well they'd never get in power ever. So it's always going to be between the Tories and Labour so that's that.*
> **Magenta, Black British, 22, London**

These young people felt largely ignorant about politics and political processes. When asked why they had not voted, many responded that they had not been contacted by the politicians and did not know how to vote. Others pointed out that they did not really understand what the different parties stood for. Among most there was a 'natural' tendency towards Labour but few could say why, with one saying that it was probably because it was 'fashionable'. As one soon to be voter explained:

> **Interviewer:** *Do you think you'd vote if you were old enough?*
> *I'm not sure. I doubt it because I don't know very much about the government, the Labour, the Conservatives ... I don't even know what it's all about. I don't know what it's all about. I don't know what they're for or against, but I'd just go with the flow I suppose. I don't think I would vote actually, no, if I had that opportunity, I don't think I would.* **Janette, Afro-Caribbean, 18, London**

# Ways forward

## Findings

The above findings confirm that, especially for these young people, politicians and decision-makers face a huge challenge if they want to restore trust, encourage participation and draw on young people's potential to contribute to civil society.

While honouring pledges and delivering specific outcomes, currently seen by governments across the world as central to restoring citizens' trust, is clearly a starting point, the young people involved in the Real Deal do not see it as sufficient. This is partly because many find it difficult to have faith in official statistics.

> *Don't take notice of these charts, like of unemployment and that, they always go by the statistics and I don't believe in them.* **Mandy (Durham)**

Direct contact between citizens and those in government is another essential condition.

'They don't know fuck-all about real life' was a common complaint of the young people in this consultation, exacerbated by the feeling that politicians often use complex and inaccessible language.

Some, however, had been pleasantly surprised when, on the occasions they had met politicians, they had found them to be 'real people'. Lisa from the Durham group discussed Chris Mullin, her local MP.

> Cos he talks to you, not at you, he talks with you and listens to you. He doesn't fob you off. He tells you what's been happening and I think he is very honest about things happening in the Houses of Parliament and the House of Lords. He was honest and open and on our level. He was a really hard worker and down to earth.

A similar reaction took place among some of the young people who attended the Real Deal Downing Street seminar. As one member of the Edinburgh group explained:

> We were expecting him [David Blunkett] to give us politician's answers for everything – maybes and incisive grumbles and all sorts of crap – but he was quite straight with us and even borderline criticising.

Involvement in specific and local issues also seems to be a primary route to reconnection. For example, the Hull group professed to be uninterested in politics and profoundly sceptical. On closer questioning, some revealed that they had signed petitions, others had made requests or complained about particular services, while others were involved in the management of their own youth organisation.

Overall, this experience shows the benefits that direct consultation can have. Not only does it allow politicians to understand better the effects of their policies, it also allows those consulted to feel that their views are being listened to and taken seriously. 'But the good thing was that they listened to us as well and most of them were taking notes as we were talking – they were writing notes and everything.'

As one young person in the Cardiff group commented:

> Yeah, you've got this thing about politicians being all like prim and proper, no family problems and when we was at one of the meetings we were saying, like we had to go round in circles saying something about ourselves and like and who our idol was. And we had to say about our mothers and one politician turned round and said it would have to be my sister because she's a single parent mother and all her kids done really well in school and it made me realise it isn't like two parents families and stuff like that. Which was good to realise.

Although direct communication and dialogue is important, it is also important to note that the young people showed a sophisticated appreciation of the need for more than words. As the Cardiff group pointed out, when discussing the visit of local councillors to their youth club, meetings can backfire if they appear to be just for show.

> *And that's the reason why I think we are so against politicians – not against them – but the view we have got on politicians, is because we met three politicians in there before and I'm not being funny, but they never took any of our ideas into consideration.*
>
> *They refused to talk about the issues that we wanted to talk about and if we would ask them a question then he would go off on some do da thing…. I don't know what he was there for to be honest because we might as well have just talked to a brick wall.*

Many commented favourably on those politicians who had spoken to them in 'down to earth' language. They found much political debate in the media, 'mumbo jumbo and big words'. Better communication, using young people's own media and methods.

> *I think politics should be advertised, marketed. Just as we live in the world of commercial things … just like how you market cans of Coke … it should be something like that. There definitely has to be more education on it and it has to attract people. I think of politics as boring men in grey suits and big long fancy words which I can't understand.*
> **(Edinburgh)**

Using animation to help get across political messages was also suggested and although politicians should be wary of appearing self-consciously 'hip' it is clear that more could be done to reach young people through their existing channels of communications.

Other suggestions for increasing young people's participation such as telephone or Internet voting were viewed sceptically, with security concerns being uppermost. Disinclination to vote seemed to be more about ignorance (what are we voting for?) and cynicism (does it make any difference?) than about the physical difficulty of voting. Another route to reconnection, again the subject of growing debate, is introducing civic and political education into the school curriculum. Participants commented on their own lack of political knowledge and felt it would be helpful to have some sort of political education at school. This reflected a more general desire for school to tackle 'real world' issues.

The establishment of new political forums in Scotland, Wales, Northern Ireland and London offers huge new opportunities for reconnection between people and politics. But as we have seen, whether they succeed with a wider range of young people depends on changes which go far beyond simple devolution of formal political processes.

As one young person in Cardiff said:

*Coming to the Real Deal meetings is the only say we have ever had, like no one has ever asked us about politics before, no teachers, parents or anything like that. This is the only opportunity we have had to talk.*

## One to one findings

As in the group discussions, many of these young people suggested that that schools offer lessons in 'citizenship' which explain the practicalities of voting and the differences between parties. A few had recently become more interested in political questions.

*I think about it. The more people say what they want, the more likely it is to happen. And I just sat back complaining and not saying anything. That's just stupid, whining and wondering why it's not happening. So that's why I thought, "Oh, better register."*
**Adrian, White British, 22, Devon**

Another questioned why it was schools taught you historical politics but not the current political viewpoints. Although they may live in a world saturated with political comment and media interest, young people seem to want the basics and are distrustful of the media to provide them with it. For some, the language of political debate is exclusionary, with one pointing out that MPs 'talk in this language known only to themselves'.

*They could explain themselves, they could explain their policies and their ideas and where they're coming from to younger people a little bit better, because I don't think, no actually quite a few of my friends like, I know quite a few of them don't vote, and when you ask them why they really don't have any reason and it's just simply because we don't know. We don't know who represents what and what they're doing and if we did then I know that I would vote. If I knew what they were doing and I could find one that was going to benefit me then, yeah, I would vote.* **Lydia, Afro-Caribbean, 23, London**

Another person explained the problems young people had distinguishing between parties:

*Anyway, with entertainment, with music for example, you have rap music and you have R & B and you know where they're coming from, and that is what it is, it's not mixed with this and that and that is what it is. We have three major, or maybe just two major, parties now and there is no sort of straight line, you can't put into a sentence or at least I couldn't, I couldn't put into a sentence what Labour is, I don't know, and because I don't know anything about my own country's politics.* **Janette, Afro-Caribbean, 18, London**

When asked to talk about what they thought the government should do most young people spoke about a wide range of social issues. Key concerns included: homelessness, the treatment of abused children, racism and discrimination, the environment, drugs and care of people with sexual diseases. Where issues had a direct and palpable relevance some had acted.

*I have actually spoken to Gordon Brown ... That was a couple of months back and I had a chat with him about why epileptics aren't allowed to get disability living allowance and he managed to avoid the question.* **Michael, Irish, 20, London**

Despite their rejection of party politics, these young people are clearly politically motivated. The overwhelming feeling was that current frameworks and formats did not organise either political choices or the ways in which they are communicated in ways which they felt they could engage with. As one explained:

*I don't know. I'm not really into politics or support any one. I like some policies and don't like other policies. There's no one party I like all their policies, or I think they really represent me or something like that.* **Ruby, White European, 20, London**

There was some sense that young people would prefer political structures in which they could choose the issues rather than the parties. Underlying what many said was a view that if politics could be made more accessible and relevant to their experiences, they would take an interest. One person said, 'I don't intend to vote unless it's about an issue I feel directly involves me.' A number of suggestions were made as to how this could be done, politicians listening and talking to people being the most important.

*Well, I identify with what I feel applies to me and, or at least something that will apply to me, but that can be from any party, because unless I see sense in what they're doing, or I can agree with them, I'm not really interested.* **Jim, 20, London**

*Like I said I think that they should be prepared to listen to the problems, like really, really listen, I think that there should be some kind of middle body that is like direct from us, the people that need the decisions, you know, but we tell them it doesn't go to a hundred different people and get changed, edited and all that kind of thing, you know from us to them, you know we need to be given more time and attention, I think we deserve more attention, we're like tomorrow's people aren't we? ... They need to be prepared to put in a lot.* **Michael, Irish, 20, London**

*Just to get a voice. More people, more foundations to say, "This is what the youth of today think. Here you go, this is it." And then that goes to the body and then the government say this is what the youth of the country want – right now, right now, this is what they need. This is what they want. They desperately need a new [voice] for the youth.* **Adrian, White British, 22, Devon**

Openness and honesty is also respected. Among those who were more politically inclined, few felt it was easy to say what exactly could or should be done to improve society. However, they agreed that the first thing politicians should do is to talk to the people who are living through difficulty.

*Tony Blair is coming out with new ideas, he is discussing it, he is coming out to the public, he is expressing his feelings, he is trying, he is trying to change certain systems and*

*certain things, you know what I mean. He actually gives a damn as an MP. He is com-*
*ing out to the people and expressing himself and that is what I like.* **Callum, White, 24,**
**London**

## Conclusions

Despite their widespread and deeply held distrust of formal politics, these young people are motivated by a wide range of social and political issues. Their more general sense of alienation and distance from mainstream institutions and communities certainly affects their view of formal politics,
but they have specific and detailed criticisms to make.

■ Politicians use irrelevant and evasive language.

■ The distinctions between parties are difficult to perceive.

■ These young people are not ready to engage with politics unless they see it making a tangible
difference to the circumstances that they face.

■ They do not feel that they are listened to or taken seriously by politics or politicians.

■ Concentrating on achieving the basic material conditions needed to live takes a greater priority
than voting and listening to politicians.

■ Gimmicks are not appreciated, and politicians should not attempt to sound 'hip'.

■ The school curriculum should include more about practical citizenship and current political
issues.

■ Politics is not perceived to make a difference, and these young people distrust the use of
statistics.

■ The four key areas that would encourage these young people to take more active interest are:

    – Evidence that politicians are taking seriously issues which they care about, such as drugs,
    the environment and discrimination

    – Being listened to and taken seriously

    – More effective, honest and appropriate communication of facts and political messages

    – The ability to make choices about specific questions and issues rather than choosing
    between parties which can seem indistinguishable.

# Ideas for action

The Real Deal has shown both how hard it is to consult effectively with young people who really know about social exclusion, and also what a difference it makes.

The people who took part in this consultation have, between them, direct experience of the most severe forms of disadvantage, adversity and exclusion. Many have been through experiences which most of us can scarcely imagine, and all know at first hand what it means to come from a background where lack of opportunity, disengagement, distrust and prejudice govern their relationship with the wider society.

More specifically, they know at first hand what it means to go through the experiences which have been identified as key long-term risk indicators of social exclusion. These include abuse, family conflict, homelessness, unemployment, school exclusion and educational failure, teen parenthood, substance addiction and prison. Their experience of the world of work is, by and large, harsh and disjointed. There is relatively little connection between what they have learned in the education system and the skills they employ to survive economically, apart from the informal lessons gained from peer group survival and encounters with institutional authority.

Many feel that they have been let down at crucial points in their lives and that whatever support they have been offered has not fitted into any coherent framework which helps them give structure and meaning to their lives. Another inescapable conclusion is that poverty and material disadvantage have a profound and damaging effect. The pressures and risks of a market-oriented, consumer and media-driven society fall just as heavily on young people facing social exclusion, and there is no doubt that lack of income and material resources make it far harder to achieve milestones which many take for granted and exacerbate other risks to the point where they become critical.

Despite the severity of their experience and the systematic nature of the exclusion they have faced, the motivations and aspirations of this group of young people are no different from most other people's. What they want is jobs, homes, families and the chance to contribute. In keeping with the whole of the younger generation, they also want their individual differences and forms of expression to be understood and tolerated. Most of all, they want to be respected as people and understood as individuals with something to offer.

Many lack detailed knowledge about the structures and systems that influence their lives from afar. This is partly because their engagement with day-to-day life consumes most of their personal resources in one way or another, partly because they have not learned the languages and strategies necessary to engage successfully with those systems, and partly because most of their experiences have been negative. In a situation where nobody seems to be listening, it is not surprising that the response is to assume that most people don't care. The experience of developing and expressing their opinions in public was completely new to most of the Real Deal participants. As one put it, "This is the first time that I've ever had anybody really listen to me, and it's good."

Despite this absence of detailed knowledge, these young people showed a sophisticated understanding of the issues and relationships which they care about and which they see as influencing them. They have strong ideas about how school, employment and social services can be improved. Their concern is most often about the framing and delivery of support rather than specifically with the quality of its content. They are often dismissive and distrustful of professionals, and it is hard to ignore the conclusion that the ones who have made a difference are those who actually listen to and make an effort to understand them. While most public services are increasingly evaluated according to outputs which represent one slice of a person's life – exam results, job placements, medical interventions – the overwhelming impression which comes from this consultation is that these young people want to be respected and taken seriously *as whole people over time* and not just to the extent that they fit into other people's categories. The complexity and fragmentation of these different systems is a major factor in impeding the progress of young people struggling to overcome disadvantage. As one said:

> I think, I mean just getting in, I've managed to get into the system. I think there's a lot of help to be done in just getting people into it. I mean I've spent a couple of years completely outside it all, didn't exist as far as anybody was concerned. And I mean now I'm on the road to getting where I want to go. And once you get into services and you find out and connect to one thing you can connect to everything, but if you never connect to the first part then you never ever reach any of that.

If they are to find a place as people who contribute to society and offer solutions and resources rather than problems and costs, then others need to listen hard. The Real Deal has produced a host of strong and consistent recommendations for specific policy areas. But it has also helped demonstrate an urgent need to develop systems and methods of consultation which give young people a real place in debates which affect them. This is hard work, and much of the project's resources have gone into supporting its participants to develop their own views and skills to the point where they can express them forcefully. But the communities and public service frameworks which all young people grow up in should already be providing these forms of support. It is not enough to announce that we are listening and then expect young people to do the rest on their own.

The policy-makers and politicians who have been involved in the Real Deal agreed unanimously that they have gained from listening and that finding ways to integrate effective consultation into the policy-making process should be a priority. Good consultation means better policy. Better policy means better outcomes and, among other things, less wasted money. Yet organising a national consultation with these young people required an alliance between five voluntary organisations and financial support from a charitable foundation. National government structures, even if money was available, are not yet equipped to integrate sustained consultation into the formation and evaluation of policy. For example, the Policy Action Teams established by the Social Exclusion Unit to examine the issues facing disadvantaged young people have had to rely on *ad hoc* structures and relationships in order to consult young people on their proposals. Nowhere is there a national forum which can bring together consultation on the range of policies affecting young people. Government departments consult in the traditional way on specific policy programmes, like education, health, crime and so on, but young people are rarely, if ever, involved in detailed discussions.

There are promising areas of practice. Some voluntary and community organisations have developed innovative structures for consulting and involving young people. The new statutory entitlement to education for citizenship and democracy at school is a major opportunity to build on what practice there is in schools and to develop the flowering relationships between schools and local communities in which so many of the new educational opportunities can be found. Peer education is becoming an established form of educational practice, subject to the same standards of quality and evaluation that we expect from mainstream education. The involvement of adults in the education system through mentoring and volunteering programmes also creates opportunities for young people to develop their understanding of wider society and to influence community life through constructive relationships rather than the distanced and stereotypical views which so often govern community views of youth. Local government in the UK, as it gradually opens up to a new national regime, is developing and experimenting with many new forms of public involvement, including youth forums and parliaments.

But this is the beginning of the story rather than its conclusion. If all young people are to be systematically included, we need a strong commitment at every level of society to finding ways to do it and acting on the results of the dialogue. This is a long-term process. It depends on the creation of new institutional forms and infrastructures. In the end its success will depend on a cultural shift which may take fifteen or twenty years to achieve. The only major group to which the democratic franchise has not been extended during the twentieth century is children and young people. Preparing them to find solutions to the challenges of the next century depends on addressing this imbalance. It may not always depend on formal rights, although the right to be consulted about decisions which affect you is established in the United Nations Convention on the Rights of the Child. It will depend on finding effective forms of participation and learning to act on the results. If young people can learn to take responsibility for themselves under conditions as extreme as the ones described in this report, then society can learn to take responsibility for listening to them.

## Recommendations

### *Support services*

■ Welfare services should be easier to access, and different departments such as housing, social security and employment should be better linked.

■ Packages of support should be personalised, and guidance and support workers should be able to advise young people as they make progress over time.

■ Professionals, especially teachers and police, should be better trained in listening to and working with young people.

■ Schools should employ confidential counsellors whom young people could confide in. This might include counselling by peers.

■ A package of support and training equivalent to the New Deal should be available for sixteen and seventeen year olds. There should be a flexible gateway period for young people with prevocational needs.

■ Better, more accessible information should be available about opportunities and entitlements for young people.

■ Government should consider introducing support packages for young people leaving care and home and who are homeless. These should include guidance, follow-up support, peer education and rent deposit schemes.

■ Young people should be involved in evaluating the outcomes and management of support services.

■ Voluntary organisations providing support services to young people should develop more effective forms of user involvement.

## Learning

■ The curriculum should include development of practical and emotional skills which help young people to cope with the situations they face out of school.

■ Work and learning should be better integrated, and learning facilities and support should be available in a wider range of contexts.

■ Young people need better preparation and more sustained support for the transition from school to post-compulsory education.

■ Schools should be equipped to respond to problems that young people face in the rest of their lives. Social, family and educational services should be better integrated. Systems of pastoral care and support need greater priority.

## Work

■ Benefits entitlements should be suspended rather than cancelled when a young person takes up temporary work.

■ Careers guidance and work experience should be drastically improved to make them more relevant and introduced earlier in young people's educational careers.

■ The minimum wage and other in work benefits should be monitored to ensure that they do not discriminate against young people.

■ Childcare places should be more widely available. There should be ongoing support for young parents and carers.

## Supporting safe lifestyles

■ Government policy on drugs should reflect the reality of young people's lives and focus on a harm reduction model. The legalisation of cannabis should be debated widely. More accurate, relevant information about drugs should be widely available.

■ There should be a wider range of safe, interesting places for young people to socialise and learn. Young people should be involved in managing and providing services for others. Support and listening services should also be available at these venues.

■ Government should examine strategies for improving concessionary rates for young people in leisure facilities. Transport services, particularly in rural areas, should be improved.

## Politics and youth policy

■ Education for practical citizenship should be an important part of the school curriculum.

■ Politicians should find more effective, appropriate ways of communicating with young people.

■ Young people need the opportunity to participate directly in debate and decision-making over issues which matter to them.

■ Local forums for young people's participation should be supported and linked to formal consultation processes for local government and other public agencies.

■ The Scottish Parliament and Welsh and Northern Irish assemblies should develop regional and national youth forums.

■ Local MPs and decision-makers should have a role in developing more effective forms of involvement for young people, such as 'youth surgeries' and local 'youth cabinets'.

■ There should be a sustained focus on the coherence of the youth policy framework at national level and the development of local youth strategies. This means greater attention to the conjunction of education and employment policy issues with other policy areas: health, care, poverty, criminal justice, leisure and sport, community regeneration, family services. A Minister for Youth should be appointed, with primary responsibility for this coherence. This Minister should not be appointed without executive powers and administrative structures which accurately reflect the responsibility for coherence and coordination.

# Appendix: methodology

The Real Deal was a unique project, combining research and group-based work over a sustained period of eight months. These methods were combined for two main reasons.

First, sustaining the consultation over time created opportunities for in-depth consultation, developing common themes and returning to earlier questions and ideas. More conventional consultation methods, such as one-off interviews and focus groups, do not allow for this depth of consultation and analysis. Working together over several months also allowed opportunities for feedback, support for the groups in policy analysis and background material, and review of earlier session reports.

Second, many of the young people involved in the consultation, given their backgrounds and life experiences, approached the discussions with caution. Devoting time to building up trust between group workers, researchers and the young people was vital to the success and accuracy of the consultation. Although some of the groups had well-established bases in their local areas and members knew each other well, others had none of this background, and developing trust, shared understanding and communication were essential. This can only take place with sustained, regular sessions and perseverance from both workers and young people.

One of the objectives of the Real Deal was to contribute to developing the communication and presentation skills of the young people involved in the project. Sustaining group work over time was vital to achieving this aim. The extent to which it took place depended on the skills of workers, the degree of involvement of each young person and the degree of participation in presentations and public events. A large proportion of the young people felt that they gained significantly from being involved in the Real Deal in this area of development.

Many Real Deal participants were coping with huge change, uncertainty and stress in the rest of their lives. This included changes in housing status, enrolment in college and training courses, moving in and out of custody, courses of medical treatment, and starting or finishing paid work. A common feature of the lives of young people experiencing social exclusion is the degree of upheaval and uncertainty that they often face. These factors impacted on group membership (see below).

The fact that participation in group consultation over time requires a degree of stability and inclusion which many young people do not have also led to a separate strand of work, the results of which are included in this report. Fifty-three individual depth interviews were conducted with homeless young people in four locations. The young people were contacted through cold-weather projects and shelters for young homeless people run by Centrepoint in London and Devon. The interviewers asked questions based on the themes of the consultation project (see opposite). The interview transcripts were analysed in a similar way to records of group sessions, and the results are presented in the report. While many of the answers and views of young people are similar, it is important to note that they came from one-off interviews rather than from work and discussion sustained over time. One to one interview findings are clearly marked wherever they are presented.

The consultation involved around 100 young people from ten locations around the country. Some were already part of existing youth groups, but most were recruited for this project. Some young people had been involved in similar work before, but most had not.

## Recruiting the groups

The groups were recruited through Centrepoint and Save the Children Fund (SCF) projects. Both SCF and Centrepoint concentrate on working with children and young people who are socially excluded and, in addition to this, they are both aware of the need to give young people a voice in decisions that affect them. There were two Centrepoint groups in London. The groups recruited through SCF were in Aberdeenshire, Edinburgh, Durham, Hull, Oxford, Cardiff, Belfast and Derry. The young people ranged in age from fourteen to 25.

The aim was to roughly balance young men and women and this worked reasonably well in most cases. The Hull group initially had nine males and only one female member and in the Belfast group the young people were split along gender lines, but for the most part gender balance was roughly equal.

Some of the young people were already known to the group workers or to the partner organisations. Others were brought in on the suggestion of initial members, while others were attracted by advertising they saw in youth centres and other projects.

Participants were encouraged to share some information about themselves with the wider group. This included their age, gender, ethnic origin, education background, work experience and any other information they thought might be relevant, for example, whether they had children, were in relationships, had been in care or had been homeless. Most of the participants were willing to include at least some of this information and some went further and produced brief self-descriptions.

For others however, confidentiality was a high priority and they were willing to give very little beyond their age and gender. This was particularly true for those living in small, rural communities who felt they could easily be identified. The issue of labelling or stereotyping is a key concern for these young people and the discussions touched on several sensitive topics such as family, community, drugs and offending, so offering confidentiality was important. These young people were assured that real names would not be used in the published report.

## Management structure

The whole project was managed by a steering committee consisting of representatives from Pilotlight, Save the Children Fund, Centrepoint, The Camelot Foundation and Demos. A separate communications group was established to develop and implement a communications strategy. One Demos researcher provided background material, coordination and week-to-week support to the individual groups, and collated and summarised transcripts and reports as they were received. Each individual group was organised by a group worker and a research worker.

## Consultation themes

Five core themes were agreed at the start of the project. These were: leisure and social activities, community and sense of belonging, education, employment and training, and transitions to adulthood. The topics chosen were deliberately broad and covered clear policy areas as well as more personal and broader social issues. A sixth topic was to be chosen once the consultation was under way, and it was identified as government and decision-making.

Each topic was approached discretely, though with the understanding that the subjects overlapped. Demos produced a briefing paper for each topic, covering basic background material, relevant research and an introduction to current government policy in the area. The briefing papers all contained broad questions that the consultation would seek to answer as well as more detailed pointers to focus the discussion. However, the emphasis was very much on the discussions and the data they would yield, rather than on a set of 'answers'.

Most groups used the briefing papers as a starting point, if they were available at the time they were planning the work. Some group workers summarised the themes for their groups, while others circulated the papers. However, the written briefing material was aimed at workers rather than at the young people themselves. As the groups were very varied and at different stages of development, it was left largely to individual workers to interpret the material as appropriate.

## Meetings

Meetings were facilitated by a group worker and observed and transcribed by a researcher. Most meetings were taped and the researcher often took supplementary notes. The young people also produced material such as project diaries, community maps or time charts. Workers completed a session evaluation at the end of each meeting, outlining the session, recording ideas which arose and noting any personal or group development that took place.

The length and frequency of meetings varied from group to group. In order to track the development of the young people over the six-month period, groups were encouraged to meet regularly, say once a fortnight for two hours. Originally the consultation was planned to cover the equivalent of fifteen two-hour sessions over the course of the project. Many groups felt this worked well, though some preferred less frequent, longer meetings. Residentials were also held as part of the consultation process: to cover specific themes, evaluate progress and, in one case, to conclude the whole project for two of the groups together.

Most groups held introductory sessions, where young people could come and go as they pleased. After these introductory sessions, the young people were asked if they wanted to join the project and given an idea of the time commitment it would entail. In some cases, the group workers needed to provide high levels of support and intensive group work in the early stages, before moving on to discussions. Most found that the young people were very enthusiastic about the project and understood its aims clearly, but they were often wary about revealing too much in the early stages. The emphasis on skills development was also important in 'selling' the idea of the meetings to the young people. As one of them put it, 'It was good that you didn't just come in and interview us and then go away.'

Because of the unpredictability and importance of other issues in the young people's lives (see above) group workers had to be flexible about people's attendance, punctuality and level of commitment. Most groups had some small change of membership, though a 'core' group also emerged in several cases. These core groups displayed a high level of commitment and a sense of ownership of the project. Some volunteered to become involved in extra activities connected with the project and, in some cases, sought to continue their groups after the project had finished.

Most group workers endeavoured to keep in touch with their groups between meetings, sending them follow-up notices, reminders and sometimes photos from events. Once analysis started, all young people were asked to review project summaries to ensure they were not being misquoted. This connection between meetings helped to make the project an ongoing concern for the young people and contributed to its success.

Group members were paid a nominal amount for their attendance in order to cover their expenses. This was felt to be important in attracting members to the project initially but, while welcome, many group workers commented that it was generally not the reason why people stayed with the project to the end. The young people were also often fed at the meetings, which again helped with maintain a level of commitment and had the added bonus of turning the meetings into something of a social event, which many young people said they had looked forward to.

Group work was structured so that the young people gradually built up their confidence and skills in expressing their ideas publicly. Researchers and group workers drew on a variety of participatory consultation techniques to support participants to express their views. Examples included getting people to write self-descriptions, young people 'designing' a leisure centre and role plays. Some workers chose to use free-flowing discussion as the format for consultation and generating ideas. This worked best in those groups where the young people knew each other relatively well and were used to meeting each other. In groups where young people were less used to communicating with each other in a social context, however, more focused and structured sessions worked better, contributing to the extent to which the sessions were able to address specific issues and questions on each of the consultation themes. Some groups fractured into smaller groups who sometimes worked on their own, for example, interviewing each other.

Researchers and group workers from the project were encouraged to meet one another at regular intervals. These meetings were facilitated by Demos and allowed workers to compare findings, discuss common issues and develop the project agenda.

## Events

Some Real Deal group members also took part in external events organised by the project partners. These included fringe debates at the Labour and Conservative Party conferences and a policy workshop at 11 Downing Street. The purpose of these events was to create an opportunity for the young people to present their views directly to politicians and policy-makers. It was also an opportunity for participants to work with others from groups across the UK on planning and delivering presentations and workshops on the consultation themes.

Training workshops preceded each of these major events, usually taking place over a weekend. There, the emphasis was on developing a clear set of messages from all the groups which could then be put to policy-makers. Training on presentation and communication was an integral part of these workshops, and participants were briefed on how to handle the media.

## Analysis of the material

Group discussions were taped and transcribed and the transcripts were submitted to Demos for analysis. As most groups were considering the issues in the same order, it was possible to produce summaries of the analysis relatively quickly for circulation to the groups, although for some individual groups changes to their timetable made this more difficult. This aspect of the project was felt to be important in that it gave the young people an opportunity to see what other groups were saying as well as correct any misreporting of their own group's discussions. Individual participants were anonymous and the young people were asked to choose pseudonyms. Some preferred not to do this and so are referred to simply by the group to which they belong.

After the consultation sessions were completed, the themes were drawn together and a first draft produced, which was again circulated to the participants. Given the timescales involved, some of the young people had moved on and were difficult to contact, but every effort was made to ensure that the young people's voices were accurately represented.

## Lessons learned

The size and composition of groups matters. While some remained as a whole throughout the project, several found it more useful to split into smaller groups. This was precipitated by friction in some groups. Some group workers often found the smaller groups to be beneficial in allowing everyone their chance to 'have a say'. This was particularly useful in cases where the young women were less likely to talk freely than the young men. Attention to these dynamics in planning the structure and timing of group work and preparing session plans emerged as an important issue.

Briefing papers and background material were most useful when they are available well in advance of group sessions. Different groups timetabled their discussions in different ways, requiring careful coordination of briefing, transcription and reporting.

Having a group worker dedicated to the consultation project throughout was valuable in a number of ways. Workers were responsible for building up and sustaining relationships with young people, maintaining a sense of purpose and direction, liaising with the researcher-coordinator and producing accurate and high quality reports and outputs. These responsibilities required time, perseverance and patience. Skills in facilitation, advocacy, policy analysis, project management are all useful in fulfilling them.

Flexibility over group membership is important. Roles within each group also need to be flexible, and the opportunity for young people to decide for themselves how they want to participate is vital. For example, some group members were happy to come to regular meetings, but did not want to take part in public events.

Tangible outcomes, whether a performance, a speech at a conference or planning and attending a residential are also very important. It is essential to give some sort of certificate or formal recognition at the end of the consultation, to record the achievement and thank participants for their contribution.

Clear planning of the stages and sessions of the consultation is vital. Preparation for public events was most successful when the objectives and roles of participants and workers were clear, and when preparation work had been completed in advance of the session. In some situations unstructured communication and group work was appropriate. In others, a clear focus on objectives and outputs, such as presentations or performances, was vital to achieving full potential.

It is useful to have a clear idea of themes to be discussed at the beginning so that the young people can see the project as a whole and not feel they are repeating material.

The resources needed for successful group consultation include: money (regular payment of expenses was an incentive to participation, especially in the early stages of a project), food, a regular venue which young people are comfortable with and can get to easily, recording and transcription equipment, consistent staff support and background information.

# Notes

1. Wilkinson H and Mulgan G, 1995, *Freedom's Children: Work, relationships and politics for 18-34 year olds in Britain today*, Demos, London.

2. Wilkinson and Mulgan, 1995 (note 1).

3. *Lean Democracy*, Demos Quarterly 4, Demos, London, 1994; SCF, 1995, *You're on your own*, Save the Children Fund, London.

4. Mental Health Foundation, 1999, *The Fundamental Facts: All the latest facts and figures on mental illness*, Mental Health Foundation, London.

5. Etzioni A, 1993, *The Spirit of Community: Rights, responsibilities and the Communitarian agenda*, Crown, New York.

6. Henley Centre, 1997, *Planning for Social Change*, Henley Centre, London.

7. Haskey J, 1995, 'Trends in marriage and cohabitation: the decline in marriage and the changing pattern of living in partnerships' in *Population Trends*, vol 80, 5-15.

8. SCF, 1995 (note 3); SCF, 1998, *Look Ahead: Young people, residential care and food*, Save the Children Fund, London; SCF, 1998, *Which Way Now?*, Save the Children Fund, London.

9. Dibblin J, 1991, *Wherever I Lay My Hat: Young women and homelessness*, Shelter, London.

10. Centrepoint, 1996, *Annual Statistics*, Centrepoint, London.

11. SCF, 1994, *Travelling People in West Belfast*, Save the Children Fund, London.

12. 6 P et al, 1997, *The Substance of Youth: The role of drugs in young people's lives today*, Joseph Rowntree Foundation, York; SCF, 1996, *Out of Our Mouths, Not Out of Our Heads*, Save the Children Fund, London.